A 5-SESSION STUDY FOR CHILDREN ON RUNNING THE CHRISTIAN RACE

WRITTEN BY MCKENZI FENN

www.warnerpress.com

ISBN: 1-59317-204-4

Editor: Kathleen Buehler

Design & Illustrations: Kevin Spear

Printed in USA

CONTENTS

Overview of the Unit

This book looks at some character traits of the Christian life. We have taken some of the sports in the summer Olympic games to represent those qualities. Through worship, games, snacks, and other activities, the children will learn about how commitment, focus, balance, strength, and endurance are part of living their lives for Christ.

God's Olympics has been created for use in an informal teaching/learning time. The activities are designed with multiple ages of children in mind. Learning centers are suggested for crafts, games, and snacks, while worship is designed for a total group experience.

How to Use This Resource

This unit is offered as a "break" in the routine of your ongoing children's ministry. The five individual sessions (with the option of opening and closing sessions) might be used on five consecutive days, or one day a week. Here are some times you might consider:

- During the 2008 Summer Olympics
- Midweek program
- Summer Saturday mornings
- Sunday morning curriculum "break" from regular program
- Day camp or VBS

Five Individual Sessions

Session	Olympic Game	Theme Word	Color	Key Verses
1	Track & Field	Commitment	Black	1 Cor. 9:24-25
2	Archery	Focus	Red	2 Cor. 13:11
3	Gymnastics	Balance	Green	Proverbs 4:25-27
4	Weight Lifting	Strength	Yellow	Philippians 4:13
5	Swimming	Endurance	Blue	Philippians 3:12-14

In Each Individual Session

Coaches' Corner

A short devotional and encouragement for the teacher and helpers.

Warm-Ups 9 minutes

Gathering time and opening activities—"stretches"—serve to transition the learners from their everyday surroundings and circumstances and prepare their hearts for worship, Bible study, and reflection. They also cushion the time for late-arrivers.

WARM-UPS PROVIDE AN EXCELLENT OPPORTUNITY FOR A YOUNGER CHILD TO BE PAIRED WITH AN OLDER CHILD. THE OLDER CHILD CAN HELP THE YOUNGER WITH VARIOUS ACTIVITIES.

On Your Mark! 1 minute

An opening prayer is led by the leader and echoed by the children. The chart of the prayer is at the end of this Unit Overview.

Get Ready! 25 minutes

This worship celebration service can happen in the same room as the other activities, or you can choose a special location such as a sanctuary, fellowship hall, or other large room. The nature of this service is not only child-centered, but largely child-led. The order of the worship service for these sessions is important; the same routine should be completed each time. The five components incorporated into each session include the following:

1. Ready Rap: Use this to launch the children into a time of praise and singing. You may wish to repeat the "Ready Rap" (at the end of this unit overview) a few times, gaining volume with each repetition; just be cautious to maintain an attitude of worship.
2. Processional (1–2 minutes)—Choose three or more children to help lead this introductory portion. The first child will carry a torch and a Bible (open to the appropriate passage for the day) to the front of the room and set it on the platform, stage, or table. (Or, two children could come down simultaneously—one with the torch, another with the Bible.)

   A second child will carry in a flag stating the "word of the day." Other children will bring in the colored ring for the day and an object that represents the theme, focus, or story of the session. The ring should be put on the wall or hung as you have determined ahead of time. An older learner who likes to read might read the scripture for the day. The theme song should be played during each processional for all services.
3. Singing together (7–10 minutes)—Children will help lead songs and motions.

   Prior to the first session, select six or seven songs to be incorporated throughout the unit. Select a "theme song" that will be used each session during the processional.

SUGGESTED SONGS:

- "Every Move I Make" (From self-titled CD from Willowcreek/Zonderkidz)
- "Step by Step," by Rich Mullins (During these three words in the song, ask students to stomp their feet hard on the ground.)
- "In the Secret" *(Shout to the Lord Kids! Vol. 2)*
- "Solid Rock" (Pam Andrews and Steven Taylor—*The Kids' Hymn Project*)
- "I Get Down" (*Every Move I Make* CD)
- "Joy!" (*Every Move I Make* CD)
- "Dive"—Steven Curtis Chapman

SUGGESTED COLLECTIONS:

Every Move I Make CD and DVD with motions—Willowcreek/Zonderkidz; www willowcreekassociation.com

Seeds CDs—www seedsmusic.com

Shout to the Lord Kids! Vol.1 and Vol.2—Integrity Music (The Vol. 2 CD is now titled *Shout Praises Kids: Trading My Sorrows.*)

4. Memory Verse Mania—The verses for this unit are Hebrews 12:1–2. The children will join motions with phrases, as follows in the chart at the end of this Unit Overview.
5. Introduction of Theme and Sharing of Scripture (2–3 minutes)—The "word of the day" is shared, and an older child reads the session passage. If possible use the "Joe Athlete" skit. Add a colored ring (black, red, green, yellow, and blue) in each session and link them in a form that you have determined. Attach them to the wall or foam board.
6. Bible Lesson (10–15 minutes)—Study the scripture and use the theme "object." Closing prayer and dismissal conclude the service.

GET SET! 45 MINUTES

This portion of the session involves reinforcement activities completed in centers. Children will rotate through snacks, crafts, and games in fifteen-minute suggested intervals. (Feel free to stretch the time at each station longer if you need to do so.)

Centers can be in one room or divided among three rooms depending on space. Also, learners should be divided into "huddles" to travel from center to center. Ideally, "huddles" should be multi-aged and remain the same throughout all sessions. However, children may be separated by age level depending on your church's individual needs and volunteers. Furthermore, if stations are not feasible for your congregation, complete these activities as a group, one after the other.

MULTIPLE SUGGESTIONS ARE MADE FOR CRAFTS AND GAMES; USE ONE OR MORE AS TIME ALLOWS OR DO YOUR OWN GAMES. AT LEAST TWO SUGGESTIONS ARE MADE FOR THE SNACK IN EACH SESSION. ONE IDEA IS HANDS-ON FOR THE CHILDREN TO CREATE AND EAT; THE OTHER IS LESS MESS FOR ADULTS TO SERVE TO THE STUDENTS.

GO! 10 MINUTES

This section uses application activities to equip and empower the students to use their knowledge of the lesson in everyday life. A commitment prayer is included.

CROSSING THE FINISH LINE 5 MINUTES

This final part of the session involves closing remarks and affirmation. If activities have taken place in multiple rooms of your facility, it is suggested that you return to the same location as the "Get Ready!" worship celebration for this closing activity.

SESSION TEMPLATE (OUTLINE)

Time Frame	Event	Activity	Supplies	Misc.
9 minutes	Warm-Ups!	Introduction		
1 minute	On Your Mark!	Opening Prayer		
25 minutes	Get Ready!	Worship Arts Celebration		
45 minutes	Get Set!	Stations: Snack Game Craft		
10 minutes	Go!	Application Activity		
5 minutes	Crossing the Finish Line!	Closing		

Other Important Information and Ideas

1. Sessions are planned and designed for 1.5 hours. To condense the session to 1 hour, cut 5 minutes from Warm-Ups, Get Ready, and Go! Eliminate 5 minutes from each center (15 minutes total) during Get Set!
2. Stretch the sessions to 2 hours by adding more time to each portion of the session.
3. Possibly give lanyards as name tags (one per child; could include the huddle name).

   It is strongly recommended to divide as many children as possible into huddles prior to your first session (or at the Opening Ceremony, if you are using it).

Olympic Hero Story

The life story of early twentieth-century Olympic athlete and missionary to China Eric Liddell is featured in each session. He will be introduced during Session 1. In each succeeding session, you can tell another part of his story as the children enjoy their snacks.

The source used for information for the Eric Liddell story is *Eric Liddell: Olympian and Missionary*, by Ellen Caughey (Urichsville, Ohio: Barbour Publishing, 2000). The book is part of the Heroes of the Faith series. You can find other information by searching "Eric Liddell" on an Internet search engine.

IF YOU KNOW OF A RECENT OR CURRENT CHRISTIAN OLYMPIC ATHLETE, YOU MAY WANT TO ADD OR SUBSTITUTE HIS OR HER STORY OF FAITH.

Suggestions for Opening and Closing Sessions/Ceremonies

OPENING CEREMONY

- Gather all together in one room for singing, devotions, games, and prayer.
- Introduce your theme song and other songs included in your *God's Olympics*.
- Lead devotions that focus on the unit memory verses and the themes. Talk about how the torch represents God's Word—it is a light for our path. (The torch might be a battery-operated candle or other light.)
- Choose some games from the unit that you have opted not to play during the sessions and play them now, or pick your own family-style games. (Family relays work well!)
- Have a processional with the Bible, the torch, and all the flags with "theme words" written on them (*COMMITMENT, FOCUS, BALANCE, STRENGTH, ENDURANCE*).
- Discuss church manners and how important it is to show respect for God and others during worship arts.

- Call on all children to stand together and make a line. Pass the torch from child to child until it reaches the "eternal flame"—a place you have designated to hold the torch.
- Distribute a calendar with dates and times of *God's Olympics*; be sure to include any special information (swimsuit for Session 5, and so on).
- Give away water bottles and/or sports accessories to each participant.

CLOSING CEREMONY

- Provide a wrap-up time for both children and parents.
- Service: Plan for all the children to help in some way with the service. Lead a meditation about the five colored rings and how they are linked together. Tie this into the importance of having all five characteristics to finish the race!
- Also, plan for children to escort the parents through the stations.

  Craft—Make bracelets or books with the five colors.

  Snack—Make a snack mix with different types of candy/snacks in these colors.

  Game—Play a game with eyes fixed on something.

RESOURCE SECTION

The following resources will be used in each session. Photocopy them as needed.

UNIT MEMORY VERSES CHART

PHRASE	MOTION
Therefore,	Point with one hand/arm in front of body
since we	Point with both hands to chest
are surrounded by such a great cloud of witnesses,	Open both arms wide
let us throw off everything that hinders	Shove out arms and flick hands in front of body, as if throwing a load into the trash can
and the sin that so easily entangles,	Cross right arm over chest and left arm across stomach (entangled)
and let us run with perseverance the race marked out for us.	Run in place
Let us fix our eyes	Take both index fingers and point to eyes
on Jesus,	Point both index fingers straight up
the author	Hold right hand up
and perfecter	Hold left hand up
of our faith,	Make a cross with both arms (right fist vertical in front of nose, left fist horizontal in front of right arm)
who for the joy set before him	Jazz hands (hands spread all the way open) by face
endured the cross, scorning it's shame,	Stretch out arms and hang head
and sat down at the right hand	Sit down (or pretend to sit down by putting hands behind body and underneath thighs)
of the throne of God.	Extend both arms up and look toward heaven
Hebrews 12:1–2	Shout it out, loud and fast

Ready Rap

Leader shouts, "Are you ready?"

Learners reply, "We are ready! We are ready! HUH!"

(On the word "HUH," students pull both arms firmly toward body, as if doing a chin-up.)

Transition Quiet Symbol

Establish a quiet signal with your students. Every time they hear this signal for the rest of *God's Olympics*, they will know to freeze, be quiet, and wait for instructions. Examples:

Teacher: Listen Up, Listen Up!

Students: Way up!

OR

Teacher holds pretend "torch" in the air and waits for all children to hold pretend torch in the air also.

OR

Blow a whistle in a rhythmic pattern of your choice; kids should echo by clapping.

Opening Prayer

Teacher	Students
Dear God,	Dear God,
please help us	please help us
keep our eyes	keep our eyes
fixed on Jesus.	fixed on Jesus.
May we please	May we please
have commitment,	have commitment,
focus,	focus,
balance,	balance,
strength,	strength,
and endurance.	and endurance.
We need you!	We need you!
And we love you!	And we love you!
In Jesus' name we pray,	In Jesus' name we pray,
Amen.	Amen.

Session 1: Track & Field (Running)

Key Word: Commitment

Session Focus: We Will—Let us run God's race!

Session Verses: 1 Corinthians 9:24–25

"Do you not know that in a race all the runners run, but only one gets the prize? Run in such a way as to get the prize. Everyone who competes in the games goes into strict training. They do it to get a crown that will not last; but we do it to get a crown that will last forever."—1 Corinthians 9:24–25

Session Materials:

Warm-Ups (Choose one of the following)

- ❏ Stretch A: banner, paper plates and washable paint, markers, baby wipes
- ❏ Stretch B: newsprint or butcher paper (one sheet for each child), pencils, scissors, tape

Get Ready! (Worship Arts)

- ❏ Processional: torch, Bible, shoe, banner/flag with *COMMITMENT* on it in black letters
- ❏ Memory Verse Mania: pictures of motions or power point with words (optional)
- ❏ Joe Athlete Skit: a gallon of water, an extra pair of shoes, a box of cookies, a jacket, knee pads, a backpack, and a pillow, black Olympic-style ring (tape if sticking to wall)
- ❏ Bible Lesson: Bibles, variety of slip-on shoes and one pair of tennis shoes, a pretend crown (or other small prize)

Get Set!

Games (Choose one of the following; instructions at end of session)

- ❏ Game A (Dizzy Lizzy): two plastic bats or similar size stick
- ❏ Game B (Pile-o-shoes): none (only shoes from learners)
- ❏ Game C ("Feet"-ball): tennis balls and chairs

Crafts (Choose one of the following; instructions at end of session)

- ❏ Craft A (Crown Creations): crown pattern, session memory verse on a mailing label, crown pattern on card stock (two per child), scissors, markers, crayons, sparkly stickers, stick-on jewels, glittery crayons/metallic markers (optional)
- ❏ Craft B (Snazzy Shoelaces): brightly colored fabric markers or permanent markers; one pair of shoelaces per child; paper plates or paper towels

Snacks (Choose one of the following; instructions at end of session)

- ❏ Snack A (Commitment Crunch): Gatorade; large bowls, scoops for each bowl, square cereal such as Cinnamon Toast Crunch or Golden Grahams; pretzel rods; bear-shaped graham crackers; marshmallows; sealable plastic bags
- ❏ Snack B (Shoe Snacks): Gatorade; shoestring licorice or Twizzler Pull-n-Peels

Go!

Closing: paper cross; markers or pens, Eric Liddell story

Crossing the Finish Line!

Crepe paper

Coaches' Corner

As you begin this journey, pray that the Lord would change the lives of your students as a result of their experience through *God's Olympics*. Also pray that the Lord would open your eyes and ears—may your life be changed as well. Commitment is something our society takes lightly; God, however, does not. May your commitment to Christ be more than casual; may your dedication to the Lord be deep!

Warm-Ups

1. During this introduction time, be sure to select three to five willing children to help with worship arts. Choose one person to carry in the torch, one to carry in the open Bible, one to carry in a running shoe, one to carry in the black ring, and one to carry in the commitment banner. Explain to the children that they will enter the room one at a time when the theme song plays. If you have enough space and volunteers to practice, go for it! If not, set up the students for success by positioning them in a location where they can see the worship arts leader and wait for his or her nod. Last, if you have an older learner who would be willing to read scripture, invite him or her to be involved as well.
2. Choose a Stretching Exercise from the end of the session to use at this time.

Transition to Worship Arts

When the Warm-Ups have concluded, ask the learners to help clean up if necessary. When you are ready to begin worship arts, give the quiet signal you have selected (see Overview of the Unit: Transition Quiet Symbol), and wait for learners' attention.

Say, **In just a few minutes we will spend some very special time with God. So for the next few seconds, we need to be totally silent. I have a special job for each of you. As we go to our spots for worship arts, think of as many kinds of shoes as you can.** Lead learners to worship arts, encouraging them to think of as many shoes as possible. Softly ask guiding questions such as, **What kind of shoes do you wear outside? to the beach? to church? to gym class?**

On Your Mark!

Recite the echo prayer, with the teacher saying a word or phrase and the students repeating:

Dear God, *(echo)* please help us *(echo)* keep our eyes *(echo)* fixed on Jesus. *(echo)* May we please *(echo)* have commitment, *(echo)* focus, *(echo)* balance, *(echo)* strength, *(echo)* and endurance. *(echo)* We need you! *(echo)* And we love you! *(echo)* In Jesus' name we pray, *(echo)* Amen. *(echo)*

REMEMBER TO GET YOUR WORSHIP ARTS ASSISTANTS READY AT THE BACK OF THE ROOM.

Get Ready! (Worship Arts)

1. Ready Rap!—Upon completion of the prayer, teach the "Ready Rap!"

   Leader: "Are you ready?"

   Students: "We are ready! We are ready! HUH!" (Pull arms firmly toward body, as if doing a chin-up.)

   Remind students that we want to show God our very best respect. Explain that they will get to be loud and crazy sometimes, but they need to be still, quiet, and calm sometimes too. Reiterate that now is a calm, quiet time.

2. Processional—Play the unit theme song and motion for the torch and Bible to be brought down and placed at the front. Then, motion for the shoe to be brought, and finally the flag/banner.

ASK THE LEARNERS TO REMOVE THEIR SHOES. INSTEAD OF CLAPPING HANDS, LEARNERS CAN CLAP THE BOTTOM OF THEIR SHOES TOGETHER.

3. Singing —Prior to the session, choose four or five songs from your prearranged song list, and then decide in which order to sing the songs. Put your CDs in order or arrange time to practice with your musicians. Either way, be sure to invite some older learners to help lead singing and motions. Suggested songs for this session: "Solid Rock," "Every Move I Make," "Step by Step," "In the Secret."

4. Memory Verse Mania—During the initial introduction to the unit memory verses, the worship arts leader may choose to guide the children in a call and response. Be sure to include the motions with the verses. (See Overview of the Unit.) You may opt to have the words available where everyone can see; be sure to include pictures that represent key words for nonreaders.

   Memory Verses: Therefore, *(echo)* since we *(echo)* are surrounded *(echo)* by such *(echo)* a great cloud of witnesses, *(echo)* let us throw off *(echo)* everything that hinders *(echo)* and the sin that so easily entangles, *(echo)* and let us *(echo)* run with perseverance *(echo)* the race *(echo)* marked out for us. *(echo)* Let us *(echo)* fix our eyes *(echo)* on Jesus, *(echo)* the author *(echo)* and perfecter *(echo)* of our faith, *(echo)* who for the joy set before him *(echo)* endured the cross, *(echo)* scorning its shame, *(echo)* and sat down *(echo)* at the right hand *(echo)* of the throne of God. *(echo)* Hebrews 12:1–2 *(echo)*

5. Introduction of Theme and Sharing of Scripture—Use the skit, if possible, to introduce and emphasize the theme. If not possible, use the other option. *(Skit is on the next page.)*

6. Bible Lesson—The children will need their Bibles. You will want to gather several of the following shoes: slippers, moon boots, boots, clogs, flip-flops, shower shoes, high heels, ballet slippers, men's dress shoes, cleats, flippers, clown shoes, and so on. Be sure to have a pair of running shoes!

   Introduce the Bible lesson. Say, **As you came to worship arts today, you were asked to think of different shoes. I wonder if any of these shoes crossed your minds. When I show you a pair of shoes, if you thought of that kind of shoe, I want you to cheer.**

   Show the shoes you have gathered, showing the pair of running shoes last. Say, **We heard some verses a few minutes ago. What were those verses about?** Running. **Today we will be talking about what running can teach us about commitment.**

DEPENDING ON TIME, AGE OF LEARNERS, AND ABILITY OF LEARNERS, YOU MAY WISH TO MARK THE BIBLES AT THE BEGINNING OF 1 CORINTHIANS AND THEN GUIDE THE LEARNERS IN FINDING ONLY THE CHAPTER AND VERSE.

   Find the scripture. Give the learners a few moments to open their Bibles to the New Testament. Then turn about halfway to the end of the Bible to 1 Corinthians. Allow the older learners to help the younger learners find chapter 9 and verses 24–25. Be sure they are in the text and looking at the scripture.

   Read and explain the scripture. Read the verses out loud. Say, **In a race all the runners run, but how many get the prize?** Affirm that there is only one winner at the end. **If you want to win the race, what do you need to do to be ready? Should you just show up at the race and hope you are the fastest runner?** There will be varied responses. **What does the Bible say should happen if you are competing in a race or game?** Highlight the portion of verse 25 that states, "Everyone who competes in the games goes into strict training." Discuss what happens during strict training: regularly scheduled practices, lifting weights, running with others, tracking progress, eating correctly, drinking lots of water, meeting with a trainer, having the right equipment, having self-control and self-discipline. Commitment is essential.

WITH JOE ATHLETE:

[The worship arts leader introduces his or her friend, Joe Athlete. Joe comes up the aisle bogged down with a gallon of water, an extra pair of shoes, a box of cookies, a jacket, kneepads, a backpack, and a pillow. He attempts to run but can't go very fast. He finally arrives at the front.]

Worship arts leader: Whatcha up to?

Joe: I'm training to run a marathon.

Worship arts leader *[stunned]*: Why are you carrying so much stuff?

Joe *[touches items as he explains]*: The gallon of water is in case I get thirsty, the extra pair of shoes is in case I wear out my current pair. I have cookies for a snack, a jacket if I get cold, kneepads in case I fall, a backpack in case I want to stop and buy anything along the way, and a pillow in case I need to rest.

Worship arts leader *[applauding him]*: You are really prepared!

Joe: I want to be prepared and ready, because I am really committed to running.

Worship arts leader: Wow, Joe! We are talking about commitment today here at God's Olympics! I think it is great that you want to have commitment. But did you know that you can have commitment without all that stuff?

Joe *[amazed]*: Really? I had no idea.

Worship arts leader: In fact, Hebrews 11:1 says to "throw off everything that hinders us!"

Joe *[drops his jaw]*: You mean I really don't need all this stuff? *[He starts throwing the items out of the way. When he is almost finished, he stops abruptly.]*

How will I have commitment if I don't have all this stuff?

Worship arts leader: You don't need stuff to have dedication and loyalty; having commitment means that when you make a promise you stick to it. Having commitment also means you have self-control. Don't worry, Joe. You will know more about having commitment by the end of the day.

[The worship arts leader calls the volunteer with the black ring to bring it to the front. Then invite a child to come up and read 1 Corinthians 9:24–25. Pray together before beginning the Bible lesson.]

WITHOUT JOE ATHLETE:

- If you cannot have Joe Athlete, invite children to bring up the various items mentioned in the skit. The worship arts leader will then begin to pick up some of the items and ask, **Do you see all this stuff? If I were going to be committed to running, all this stuff would help me, wouldn't it? I'd need to carry it with me as I ran, right?** The children should respond with no. The worship arts leader will then say, **Well, then, what do I need to show I'm committed?**
- Call an older child or adult volunteer to the front with the black Olympic-style ring. After displaying it on the stage, he or she will point to the banner with the word *COMMITMENT* on it. Let the child explain: "Today our theme is commitment. This word means dedication and loyalty; having commitment means that when you make a promise you stick to it. Having commitment also means you have self-control. Today we will be talking about commitment to God."
- Call up another child to read 1 Corinthians 9:24–25 from the open Bible brought forth during the processional.
- Pray as soon as the passage is finished.

Now ask the students to read verse 25 again. Ask, **If I run in the Olympics, win a gold medal, and become a famous athlete, do I get to take my medal with me to heaven?** No. **The Bible says we go into strict training to get a "crown that will last." What do you think this sentence means?** Allow responses. Explain that we need commitment to experience eternal life. **Whom or what should we be committed to if we want to experience eternal life? Jesus Christ.**

Ask, **If you are committed to Jesus Christ, what kinds of things do you do to know him better?** Spending time alone with God, listening for God, reading the Bible, praying, worshiping, singing songs of praise, sharing his love with others, going to church and being with other believers, and so on.

IF YOU HAVE A HIGH SCHOOL STUDENT WHO RUNS FOR A TEAM OR A FORMER TRACK STAR IN YOUR CHURCH, YOU MIGHT INTERVIEW HIM OR HER FOR TWO MINUTES TO ACCENTUATE WHAT STRICT TRAINING ENTAILS. KEEP IT BRIEF.

Illustrate the lesson. Ask five children to compete in a race. Give four children shoes that slip on easily; give one child a pair of running shoes—with the laces tied tightly. (Be certain the child cannot slip easily into the running shoes.) Explain that the students are racing to see who can put the shoes on the fastest. Say, **On your mark! Get ready! Get Set! Go!** Give a paper or toy crown or other small prize to the winner.

Ask, **If these five people were going to run a ten-mile race, and all of them had strict training but were wearing these exact shoes, who would most likely win?** Ask why each pair of slip-on shoes would not be a good choice. Illustrate that the flippers could make blisters, high heels could make you fall, and so on. When the children respond that running shoes would be best, say, **They take too long to put on your feet. They're too hard to wear. I don't have time to fool with that extra work. What do you think?** Wait for responses and then ask the learners if they can make a connection between wearing running shoes and being committed to Christ. The responses may amaze you! Say, **Just as you choose which shoes are going to support you all day long, you have to choose your foundation for life: Jesus.**

Conclude the lesson. Remind the children that in a race, only one person wins. Ask the learners how many people can win in God's race, and reinforce that everyone can win in God's race! Say, **So, every time you put on your running shoes this week, remember that you can run God's race! Every time you see running shoes, remember that you can have commitment to God!** Challenge the learners to run God's race and to go into his training program. Ask all the children who are willing to run God's race to chant repeatedly, "Let us run God's race!"

Pray together. Use an echo prayer: Dear Jesus, *(echo)* thank you *(echo)* for teaching us *(echo)* about commitment. *(echo)* Help us *(echo)* be committed *(echo)* to you. *(echo)* Amen.

7. Dismiss the learners by huddles and send groups directly to "Get Set!" stations. If you are not rotating through stations, dismiss the learners by rows and send them to whichever activity they will complete first.

GET SET!

The learners will spend approximately 15 minutes in each station. If you are traveling from room to room, allow 12–13 minutes for the activity and 2–3 minutes to transition.

STATION 1: GAMES

The games today are relays. Explain that these relays will all teach something about running God's race. Choose one or more games from the end of the session, or substitute your favorite relays. Encourage the younger learners and older learners to work together.

STATION 2: CRAFTS

Choose one of the crafts from the end of the session to highlight in this station.

STATION 3: SNACKS

Choose one of the snacks from the end of the session. The two suggestions differ in involvement of the students in preparing the snack. In addition to either snack, serving Gatorade or another sports drink would be a fun treat.

As the children eat the snack, read the following paragraphs about Eric Liddell, a former Olympian and a missionary:

As Eric Liddell of Scotland grew up, sports were a big part of his life. His two favorite sports were running and rugby. At college, Eric had to make a choice between the two sports, and he chose running. He was an excellent runner and began training for the Paris Olympics on Great Britain's team. Eric's best running event was the 100-meter race. The critics and fans thought Eric would win this race at the Olympics.

But after he had made the British Olympic team, he found out that the 100-meter race was going to be run on a Sunday. Eric refused to run on Sunday, because that was a day to worship God. Eric's most important race was his race for the Lord. On that Sunday, he went instead to a church in Paris and preached to the people. Many people from Scotland and the rest of Great Britain were upset with him. They couldn't understand. They felt as if he had let his country down. But Eric was committed to following God, no matter what.

We will learn more about this Olympic athlete in the next session.

IF YOU SEARCH "ERIC LIDDELL" ON AN INTERNET SEARCH ENGINE, YOU WILL FIND MORE INFORMATION ABOUT HIM.

GO!

1. Upon completing the three stations, learners should all come together in one large group. Recite the "Ready Rap" again to get everyone refocused and transition to the closing portion of the session.

2. Ask the students to close their eyes and to think of what they learned today about running God's race. Say, **Open your eyes. I need someone to share with me one new thing you learned about God today.** Take several responses; this activity offers you a chance to affirm your students and politely refocus any misperceptions you may hear.

3. Ask the students to shout the key word of the day: *COMMITMENT.* Then say, **The most important commitment we can make is to Jesus Christ. And the most important race we can run is God's race. If you want to make a commitment to run God's race, I want you to sign your name on this cross.**

Hang a brown paper cross on the wall near the silhouettes or banner from the Warm-Ups activity (silhouettes should be running toward the cross). Allow the children time to sign the cross if they choose. Be sensitive to those who are not yet ready to commit to running God's race; promise to pray for them as they consider this important step.

Crossing the Finish Line!

1. Break the tape. You will need three-foot strips of crepe paper (one per child). Instruct the children to get in groups of three. Give each child a piece of crepe paper. Ask two learners to hold the crepe paper—one child at each end—and stretch it loosely. The third learner should run through the tape and shout, "I will run God's race!" Take turns until all learners have had a chance to break the tape.

2. Close with prayer. Ask for a child to close the group in prayer. (If the child struggles, whisper words in his or her ear to be repeated.)

3. Dismiss. Distribute any information sheets about the next session and dismiss the children according to your church procedures.

Resource Section

Stretching Exercises (Choose One)

Stretch A: Shoe Stamping

Materials needed: banner, washable paint on paper plates, markers, baby wipes

To eliminate much of the cleanup, you may want to bring some old shoes from home to use instead of allowing the children to use their own shoes.

Prior to the session, write *Let us run God's race!* on a butcher paper banner in large letters. Learners should remove one or both shoes. Be sure to tuck the shoelaces inside the shoe! Use the shoes as "stamps" and carefully dip the bottom of a shoe into the washable paint. Then press the sole of the shoe in different places on the butcher paper banner. Learners can stamp randomly on the paper, or they might stamp on top of the letters so their shoe prints spell *Let us run God's race!* Instruct the children to clean the shoes with baby wipes.

Stretch B: Silhouette Shapes

Materials needed: a sheet of newsprint or butcher paper for each child, pencils, scissors, tape

Learners will pair up with a partner. Give each child his or her own sheet of butcher paper. Instruct the learners to lie down on their sides on the paper in a running position. Learners should take turns tracing each other on the paper. Be certain that all silhouettes are facing the same direction. Once children are finished tracing, help them cut out their silhouettes and hang them on the wall.

Station 1: Games (Choose One)

A. Dizzy Lizzy

Prep: Gather two plastic bats or similar size sticks.

Steps: Divide learners into two teams. Each team should stand in a straight line. Several feet away from the learners, place one bat at the end of each line. Each learner should do the following things on his or her turn: run to the bat, hold the bat upright and bend over and place forehead on the top (so person is looking at the floor), walk ten circles around the bat (keeping forehead on the bat), run back to the team and tag the next player, and then go to the end of the line. The team to finish first wins.

Spiritual Application: Say, **Sometimes it is hard to stay on the path set before us. Things can entangle us and cause us to fall down. What does Hebrews 12:1–2 say about things that bog us down?** Get rid of them. Discuss what these things might include: cheating, lying, gossiping, watching bad movies, stealing, not sharing, saying mean things. **What can we do to help us stay straight with our commitment to Christ?** Read the Bible, be quiet before God, pray, talk to a trusted adult, tell a friend about Jesus. Recite the unit memory verse with motions.

B. Pile-O-Shoes

Steps: Divide the learners into two teams. Each team stands in a team circle. All players should remove their shoes and place them in a pile in the center of the team circle. Mix up the shoes so that no pairs are together. Each player should do the following things on his or her turn: find his or her own shoes in the pile, put them back on, return to her or his place, and tag the person on the left. Choose a player from each team to go first. Continue clockwise until all the learners are again wearing shoes. The team to finish first wins.

Spiritual Application: Ask the learners what our running shoes teach us about God. Review from the worship arts celebration that we can choose our shoes, and we can choose to be committed to God.

C. "Feet"ball

Prep: Provide one tennis ball and two chairs per team.

Steps: Divide the learners into even teams. Each team lines up behind a chair. The other chair is placed a few feet away. On your signal, the first player puts the ball between his or her feet. The object is to jump—with the ball between the feet—from the starting chair point, to and around the far chair, and then back to the team. The remaining team members do the same thing until all players have finished. If the ball is dropped or slips out from between the feet, the player must go back to a chair. Variations: Play by the same rules but with different objects: book on the head, beanbag on the foot, spoon on the nose, balloon between knees, fruit between elbows.

Spiritual Application: When we get off the path and lose it, we should go back and try again. God will forgive us when we ask. Stress to the learners that it is never too late to try again. Additionally, being committed to Christ also involves focus, balance, strength, and endurance. Explain that we will be talking about these other things in the next few sessions.

IN ANY RELAY, YOUNGER LEARNERS CAN BE PAIRED AS PARTNERS WITH OLDER LEARNERS AND BOTH CAN COMPLETE EACH TASK TOGETHER. ANOTHER OPTION WOULD BE TO HAVE THE YOUNGER LEARNERS COMPLETE A RELAY TOGETHER WHILE THE OLDER LEARNERS CHEER THEM ON, AND THEN VICE VERSA. REINFORCE THAT WE NEED TO ENCOURAGE ONE ANOTHER IN OUR COMMITMENTS TO CHRIST.

STATION 2: CRAFTS (CHOOSE ONE)

A. CROWN CREATIONS

Supplies: session verses printed on mailing labels, crown pattern from Resource Section on card stock (two per child), scissors, markers, crayons, sparkly stickers, stick-on jewels, glittery crayons/metallic markers (optional)

Steps: Make copies of the crown pattern in the Resource Section. Decorate the crowns with markers and stickers before cutting them out of the card stock. Connect the ends of the crown around each child's head and then staple each crown for individual size. Add the mailing label with the scripture memory verse. Encourage the older learners to read the memory verse to the younger learners. Variations: Crowns can also be made by cutting a piece of construction paper or card stock vertically down the middle with a wavy cut. Match up the ends of both pieces of paper and staple.

B. SNAZZY SHOELACES

Supplies: brightly colored fabric markers or permanent markers; one pair of light-colored shoelaces per child; paper plates or paper towels

Steps: Give each child a pair of shoelaces and a paper plate. Write the child's name on the paper plate to identify laces later. Direct the learners to decorate the laces with the markers. They might write *Run God's race!* on the laces. As the students are working, discuss commitment to Christ and what that means. Reinforce that we must choose to be committed to Christ, and that the extra effort of studying our Bible, going to church, and praying to God are worth it! Let the shoelaces dry (if painted) and send them home with the students at the end of the session. Remind the students that these laces are a reminder to run God's race!

STATION 3: SNACKS

A. MAKE: COMMITMENT CRUNCH

Ingredients: square cereal such as Cinnamon Toast Crunch or Golden Grahams; pretzel rods; bear-shaped graham crackers; marshmallows; sealable plastic bags

Steps: Place each ingredient in a large bowl and set the bowls in a line on the table. Tell the learners that they will be making "Commitment Crunch." Each ingredient represents one way we can be committed to Christ. The square cereal reminds us to read our Bibles, the pretzels represent prayer, and the graham crackers remind us to "bear" one another's burdens. The marshmallow will represent another way to practice commitment to Christ that the children will choose. Give the students sealable plastic bags and instruct them to take a small handful of each ingredient. While scooping the ingredient into the bag, each child should say, "Reading my Bible helps me to be committed to Christ"; "Praying helps my commitment to Christ"; "Bearing one another's burdens helps me to be committed to Christ"; and "(child fills in the blank with own idea) helps me in my commitment to Christ."

B. SERVE: SHOE SNACKS

Offer the children shoestring licorice or Pull-n-Peel Twizzlers to reinforce running in God's race!

Crown Pattern

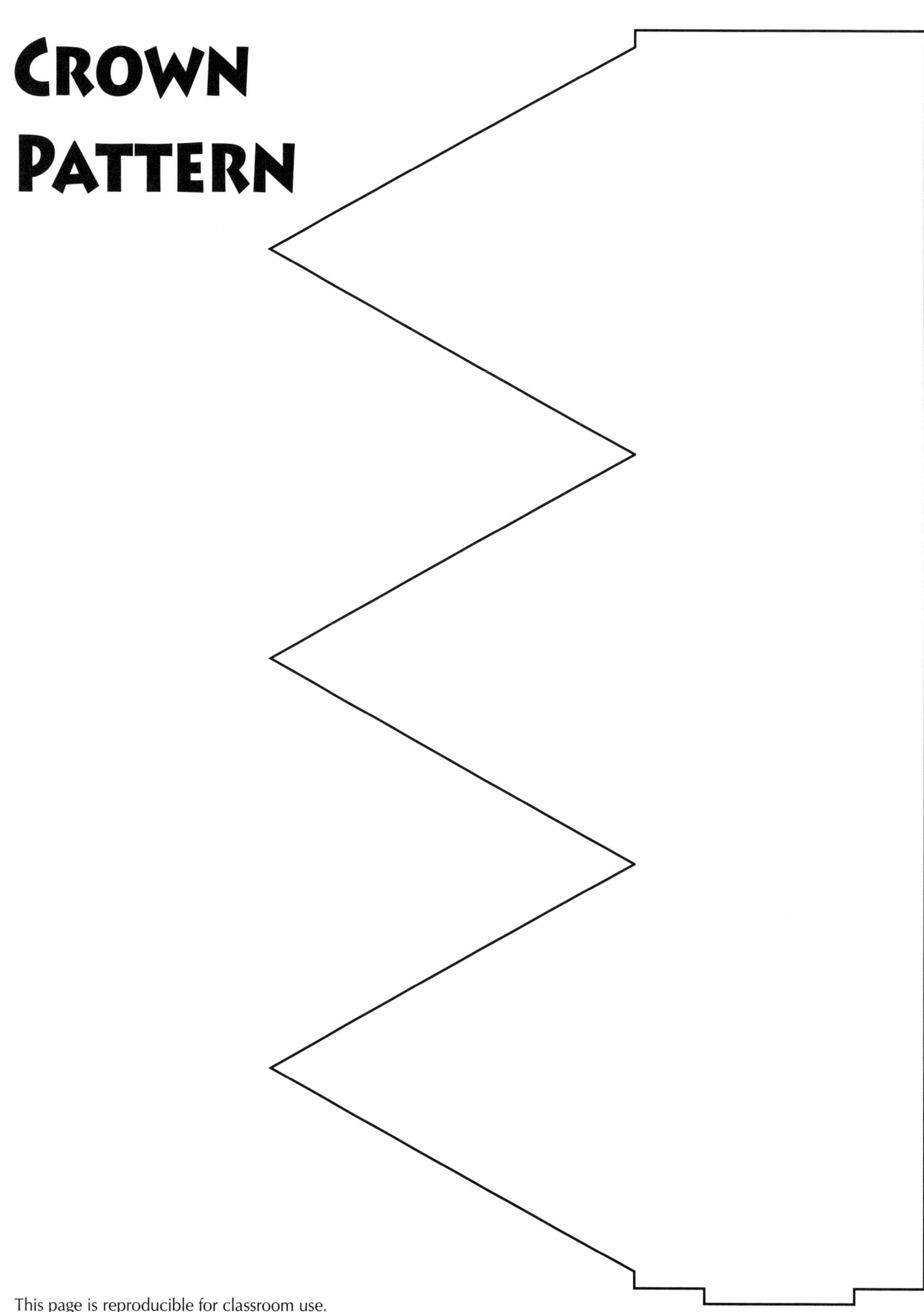

Session 2: Archery
Key Word: Focus
Session Focus: Let us fix our eyes on Jesus!
Session Verse: 2 Corinthians 13:11

AIM FOR PERFECTION, LISTEN TO MY APPEAL, BE OF ONE MIND, LIVE IN PEACE. AND THE GOD OF LOVE AND PEACE BE WITH YOU.— 2 CORINTHIANS 13:11

Session Materials:

Warm-Ups (Choose one of the following)

- ❑ Stretch A (Staring Contests): none
- ❑ Stretch B (Magic Eyes): 3-D picture book, picture, poster or calendar
- ❑ Stretch C (Bright Objects): several "bright" objects (star-shaped light, shapes cut from neon poster board and a flashlight to shine on them)

Get Ready! (Worship Arts)

- ❑ Processional: torch, Bible, banner/flag with the word *FOCUS* in red letters, large bull's-eye target
- ❑ Memory Verse Mania: pictures of motions or power point with words (optional)
- ❑ Joe Athlete Skit: toy bow and arrow, red ring (tape if sticking to wall)
- ❑ Bible Lesson: beanbags, foam balls, or other small item to toss

Get Set! (Supplies vary)

Games (choose one of the following; instructions at end of session)

- ❑ Game A (Bean Bag Toss): bean bags, buckets or targets
- ❑ Game B (Target Toss): premade target (felt and markers), premade Velcro Ping-Pong balls
- ❑ Game C (Mr. Target): butcher paper, felt shapes, Velcro and Ping-Pong balls

Crafts (choose one of the following; instructions at end of session)

- ❑ Craft A (Target Magnets): Fun Foam sheets or thin sponges, cross and arrow patterns from Resource Section, pens, self-adhesive Velcro, magnetic strips, scissors
- ❑ Craft B (Masks): two- to three-inch cross pattern from Resource Section, paper plates, yarn, scissors, hole punch, crayons or markers

Snacks (choose one of the following; instructions at end of session)

- ❑ Snack A (Tasty Targets): pita bread and pizza sauce, tortillas (or round chips) and salsa, mini bagels and cream cheese, or round crackers and spray cheese
- ❑ Snack B (Rounds): any round cookie or cracker

Go!

- ❑ Large paper cross used in worship arts, paper arrows

Crossing the Finish Line!

- ❑ Bull's-eye target with a cross in the middle

Coaches' Corner

Have you ever shot a real bow and arrow? Sometimes it leaves big bruises on the side of your arm. Ouch! Have you ever faced a time in your walk with the Lord when even though you were focused on him and aiming to be like Christ, you were bruised and hurt? What happens when you don't focus on the Lord? What about when your eyes appear to be focused on him, but the rest of your life doesn't align itself with Christ? Aiming for perfection (to be like Christ), as the scripture states, is a daunting task. But it is one that is worth any pain we may sustain or any hurdle we may have to jump over. May you be drawn closer to the Lord and encouraged to pursue his character through the activities in this session!

Warm-Ups

1. Remember to find worship arts helpers during this time: torch bearer, Bible carrier, someone to bring in the banner, someone to carry in the red ring, a child to carry in the target, an older learner to read scripture.
2. Choose a Stretching Exercise from the end of the session to use at this time.

Transition to Worship Arts

REMEMBER TO GET YOUR WORSHIP ARTS ASSISTANTS READY AT THE BACK OF THE ROOM.

When the Warm-Ups have concluded, ask the learners to help clean up if necessary. When you are ready to begin worship arts, give the quiet signal you have selected (see Overview of the Unit) and wait for learners' attention. Remind learners to give their best respect to God during worship arts.

On Your Mark!

Recite the echo prayer (see Overview of the Unit) used last week, with the teacher saying a word or phrase and students repeating.

Get Ready! (Worship Arts)

1. Ready Rap!—Upon completion of the prayer, say the "Ready Rap!" (See Overview of the Unit.) Be sure to remind students to show God their very best respect.
2. Processional—Play your chosen unit theme song, and motion for the torch and Bible to be brought down and placed at the front. Then motion for the target to be brought to the front, and finally the flag/banner.
3. Singing—Prior to the session, choose four or five songs from your prearranged song list and then decide in which order to sing the songs. Put your CDs in order or arrange time to practice with your musicians. Either way, be sure to invite some older learners to help lead the singing and motions. Suggested songs for this session: "Every Move I Make," "Step by Step," "In the Secret."
4. Memory Verse Mania—Recite the unit memory verse with motions. (See Overview of the Unit.) Have a contest between boys and girls to see who can say the verse the loudest and strongest!
5. Introduction of Theme and Sharing of Scripture—Use the skit, if possible, to reinforce the theme. If not possible, use the other option.

WITH JOE ATHLETE:

[Joe Athlete enters with a pretend bow and arrow, blatantly staring straight ahead and ignoring everyone who calls out to him. When he gets front and center, he still stares ahead and keeps his back to the crowd.]

Worship arts leader: Joe, you okay?

Joe Athlete *[loudly]*: Yes, I am trying to stay focused. I want to keep my eyes fixed.

Worship arts leader: You want to keep your eyes fixed? Are they broken? I don't understand. What do you mean?

Joe *[emphasizing words in caps]*: Hebrews 12:1–2 says, "Therefore, since we are surrounded by such a great cloud of witnesses, let us throw off everything that hinders and the sin that so easily entangles, and let us run with perseverance the race marked out for us. LET US FIX OUR EYES ON JESUS, the author and perfecter of our faith, who for the joy set before him endured the cross, scorning its shame, and sat down at the right hand of the throne of God."

Worship arts leader *[nodding]*: I see. How do we do that? How do we keep our eyes fixed on Jesus?

Joe: I don't know. *[turns and addresses the children]* I am not sure how to keep my eyes fixed on Jesus, but I think we will all be able to answer that question at the end of the day. Our theme today is focus. I sure want to be focused on Jesus, don't you?

[Call a volunteer to link the red ring to the black ring and then read 2 Corinthians 13:11. Ask for a volunteer to pray. Begin the Bible Lesson at the conclusion of the prayer.]

WITHOUT JOE ATHLETE:

- The worship arts leader will stare over the children's heads for a few seconds. Next, the leader will put a hand above the eyes and keep on staring. Try two other actions: Rub eyes and keep staring. Squint and point in the same direction. Finally, make the motions of aiming to shoot a pretend bow and arrow. The worship arts leader asks, **What do you think I'm doing?** Allow for responses. **I'm trying to focus.**
- Repeat Hebrews 12:1–2 again for the children, this time emphasizing the words "Let us fix our eyes on Jesus."
- Call up the volunteer (child or adult) with the red ring; let him or her link it to the black ring. Then the volunteer shows the flag/banner and states, "Our theme word today is FOCUS. We will be talking about what it means to have our eyes fixed on Jesus."
- Call on another volunteer to read 2 Corinthians 13:11, the session verse.
- Pray. Be ready to begin the Bible Lesson as soon as the prayer is finished.

6. Bible Lesson—The children will need their Bibles. You will want beanbags, foam balls, or other small items to toss. You will also want a large paper cross, several paper arrows, a marker, and tape.

   Introduce the Bible lesson. Start by asking for six to eight volunteers to come forward. Give each volunteer a beanbag; each person has a turn to throw the beanbag. Don't designate any mark to aim for. Let the volunteers begin. Congratulate one person for hitting the mark, then tell the next person better luck next time. Cheer for some and apologize to others. Ignore their confusion and questions regarding the location of the target. When all the volunteers have finished, ask those who "missed the target," **Why didn't you try to hit it? In this game the target was invisible. We can't aim unless we know our focus, can we?**

   Play the game again with the target from the processional hanging on the wall. **Where did you aim this time? You knew your target. You had your focus.**

   Find the scripture. Give time for the children to find 2 Corinthians 13:11 in their Bibles. The older learners can help the younger ones.

   Read and explain the scripture. Invite a volunteer to read the verse out loud while the others follow along. Ask, **Where should we aim in our faith?** Reread the verse and reinforce the words "aim for perfection." **Who is perfect?** Jesus! **Since Jesus is the only person who ever lived a perfect life, we should aim to be like him.** Remind the learners of the unit verses from Hebrews. **We should fix our eyes, but also our whole lives, on Jesus.**

Illustrate the lesson. Throw a beanbag. Focus your eyes hard on the target but throw the beanbag off to the side. Ask, **Why didn't I hit the target? I mean, I was focused on the target! In archery, it is very important for the whole body to be lined up just right if the archer wants to hit the target. If we don't align the entire body with the target, it really doesn't matter where we look.**

Hang a large paper cross on the wall. Say, **Obviously, we need to focus our lives—not just our eyes—toward Christ. How can we fix our eyes, hearts, and lives on Jesus?** Pray, memorize scripture, read the Bible, be still with God, go to church, talk to our friends about Jesus, pray about every choice we have to make, test if something would be aiming for "perfection" with Jesus or if it would cause us to look away from God. Write these ideas down on paper arrows and invite volunteers to tape them up on the wall pointing to the cross.

Pray together. Use an echo prayer: Dear God, *(echo)* Please help me *(echo)* fix my eyes, *(echo)* my life, *(echo)* and my heart *(echo)* on Jesus. *(echo)* I *(echo)* want to aim *(echo)* toward him *(echo)* in all I say, *(echo)* in all I think *(echo),* and in all I do. *(echo)* I want to be like him. *(echo)* Amen.

7. Dismiss the learners by huddles and send groups directly to "Get Set!" stations. If you are not rotating through stations, dismiss the learners by rows and send them to whichever activity they will complete first.

Get Set!

The learners will spend approximately 15 minutes in each station. If you are traveling from room to room, allow 12–13 minutes for the activity and 2–3 minutes to transition.

IF YOU HAVE SOMEONE IN YOUR CHURCH WHO IS CERTIFIED TO TEACH ARCHERY, YOU MAY WISH TO HAVE HIM OR HER GIVE A DEMONSTRATION DURING THIS GAME TIME.

STATION 1: GAMES

Choose from one of the games explained at the end of the session. Each of these makes use of some kind of a target.

STATION 2: CRAFTS

Choose one of the crafts from the end of the session. Help the children think of what they are learning about focus today and to write a short message or the session verse on their crafts.

STATION 3: SNACKS

Choose one of the snacks at the end of the session to highlight focusing on the target. Remember to ask a child to pray before sharing in the snack!

While the students eat, share some more of the story of our Olympic hero, Eric Liddell.

Remember that last week we learned about a man named Eric Liddell. He had been selected to be on the British Olympic team for the Paris Olympics. But his best race, the 100-meter race, was going to be run on Sunday, so he told his coach and the officials that he couldn't run. He was that committed to following God.

Eric was given the opportunity to run the 200-meter and 400-meter races, which were run on a day other than Sunday. He hadn't trained as much for these long races! People all over Scotland, Britain, and the world made fun of Eric. They thought he was crazy and that he had no chance to win. But Eric had his eyes on God and what God thought of him, not on people and what they thought of him! He would run these races.

At the Olympics he ran the 200-meter race and came in third. Later in the week he ran the 400-meter race with all his heart and did his very best. Guess what happened?! Eric won the race! He earned a gold medal! And guess what else! Eric not only won the gold, but he set a brand new world record! More than the medal and the world record, the best part of the story is that Eric Liddell had his eyes fixed on Jesus. His focus was on more than a race. His focus was to follow Jesus.

GO!

1. Gather all the learners together in one large group. Recite the "Ready Rap" to get everyone refocused and transition to the closing portion of the session.

2. Cross Commitments. Draw attention to the large paper cross and the arrows that talk about things we do to FOCUS on Jesus (used in worship arts).

   Say, **This cross represents how we need to fix our eyes and lives and hearts on Jesus.** Review how to do so: talking to God about every decision to make sure it would please him, pray, go to church, and so on.

   Give each child a blank paper arrow. Explain that they will have a personal prayer time with God. They will pray about and then write down or draw a picture of how they personally are going to fix their eyes on Jesus. After a time of prayer, the children can share their responses if they want. Then ask each child to tape his or her arrow on the wall pointing to the cross.

3. Conclude by asking for volunteers to lead in prayer.

Crossing the Finish Line!

1. Fix Your Eyes on Jesus Chant. Hold up the bull's-eye target with a cross in the middle.

   Steps: Ask the children to shout out, "FIXED ON JESUS." Say, Every time I show you this bull's-eye with a cross on it, I want you to shout out, "FIXED ON JESUS." Practice a few times. Then ask the following questions and show the bull's-eye to indicate the answer. **Where are your eyes?** (show bull's-eye) **Where are your feet?** (bull's-eye) **Where are your hands?** (bull's-eye) **Where are your thoughts?** (bull's-eye) **Where are your words?** (bull's-eye) **Where are your actions?** (bull's-eye) **Where are your lives?** (bull's-eye) **Where are your hearts?** (bull's-eye)

2. Dismiss. Distribute any instruction sheets for the next session and follow the dismissal procedures for your church.

Resource Section

Stretching Exercises (Choose One)

STRETCH A: STARING CONTESTS

In twos, students will stare each other in the eyes. The first person to flinch, smile, laugh, move, and so on is out. To make it even more challenging, the first to blink is out! Consider having a double elimination tournament to see which child is the staring contest queen or king!

STRETCH B: MAGIC EYES

Materials needed: 3-D picture books or posters

Encourage the students to stare at the pictures to see if they can find the hidden images. Be sure to encourage those students who struggle to see the picture within the picture!

STRETCH C: BRIGHT OBJECTS

Materials needed: several "bright" objects (star-shaped light, shapes cut from neon poster board and a flashlight to shine on them)

Stare at one of the bright objects for one minute. Close your eyes; you should see the shadow of the object on your eyelids for a few seconds when you close your eyes. Do not stare directly into a bright light.

STATION 1: GAMES (CHOOSE ONE)

A. BEANBAG TOSS

Prep: Gather five beanbags and buckets or targets; write *Jesus* or *Perfection* on each bucket.

Steps: Establish the boundary for the start line. Arrange the buckets in a straight, vertical line, or scatter them some distance apart. (You can vary per round of the game.) Give each person five beanbags. Take turns throwing the beanbags in a bucket. You may wish to give away small prizes for each bag that goes in a bucket.

Spiritual Application: Recall the session verse to "aim for perfection." Invite the children to share different ways to focus on Jesus in their lives (read the Bible, pray without ceasing, spend time alone with God, be still, memorize scripture, and so on).

B. TARGET TOSS

Prep: Buy a large piece of felt; draw concentric circles and add the following amounts: 5, 10, 15, 25, 50; hot glue the rough section of Velcro to three Ping-Pong balls; hang the target on a wall or fence.

Steps: Establish the starting line. Each child throws three Velcro balls toward the target. Add the points for each throw and give the child the grand total. If the Velcro ball hits the line, the lower point value is granted.

Variation: Make the target out of poster board and lay it on the floor. Toss beanbags instead of Velcro balls.

Spiritual Application: Reinforce the unit and session memory verses. We fix our eyes on Jesus, just as we fixed our eyes on the target. Then we AIM for perfection, which involves our whole selves. Having focus means fixing our eyes and then aiming with our whole selves. When we don't hit the center of the target, we still kept on trying. We should still aim for perfection even when we fall short of the goal.

C. MR. TARGET

Prep: Cut a human silhouette out of paper; cut out felt pieces or other fabric where Velcro will stick—a mouth, ears, eyes, hair, hands, feet, arms, legs, and heart—and attach to the silhouette; attach the rough side of Velcro to three Ping-Pong balls.

Steps: Take turns throwing the Velcro balls at the human target.

Spiritual Application: Wherever the ball sticks, the person throwing has to name how that body part can be used to focus on Jesus and aim for perfection.

STATION 2: CRAFTS (CHOOSE ONE)

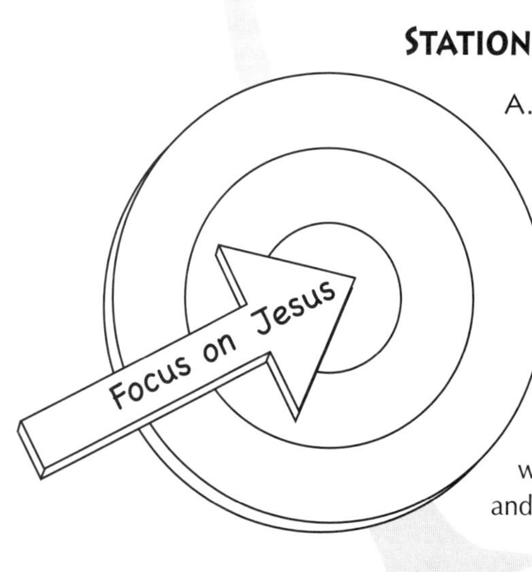

A. TARGET MAGNETS

Supplies and Prep: Make copies on card stock of the circle and arrow patterns in this Resource Section. Ahead of time use the 3-inch circle pattern to cut circles out of Fun Foam sheets or thin sponges, enough for each child to have one. Provide magnetic strips, ballpoint pens, scissors, the patterns, and small pieces of self-adhesive Velcro.

Steps: Tell the children that they will make refrigerator magnets to remind them to keep their focus on Jesus. Give each one a 3-inch foam or sponge circle. Each will place the 2-inch circle pattern inside the big circle and trace around it with a pen. Then place the 1-inch circle pattern inside the lines of the 2-inch circle and trace around it. Cut and attach one side of a small piece of Velcro inside the

1-inch circle. Draw around the arrow pattern onto the foam or sponge, and cut out the arrow. Write *Focus on Jesus* on the arrow with the word *Jesus* in the arrow point. On the back of the arrow point, attach the other half of the Velcro piece. Stick the arrow to the center of the target. Add a magnetic strip to the target back.

B. MASKS

Supplies: Two- to three-inch cross pattern from the Resource Section, paper plates, yarn, scissors, hole punch, crayons or markers

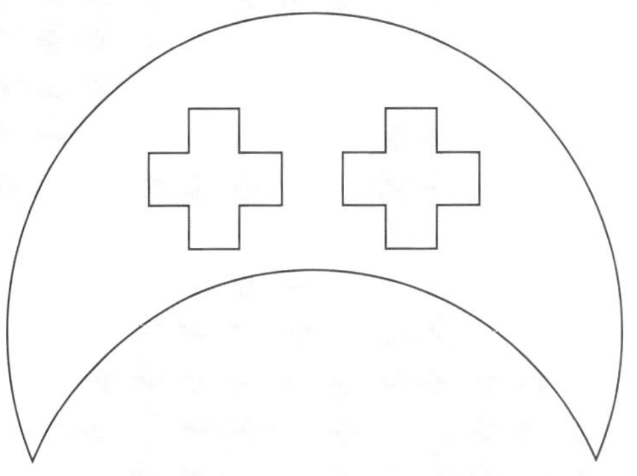

Steps: Copy the cross pattern in this Resource Section. Trace the cross pattern on the top right and top left side of a paper plate. (See illustration.) Cut the paper plate under the crosses. Using a hole punch, punch a hole inside both crosses; cut out the crosses with scissors. Learners should be able to see out of the cross-shaped "eyes" in the masks. Decorate the masks with crayons and markers. Write on the masks the session verse or the words *I fix my eyes on Jesus*. Add yarn to the mask and wear over the eyes.

Station 3: Snacks (Choose One)

A. MAKE: TASTY TARGETS

Ingredients: Pita bread and pizza sauce, tortillas (or round chips) and salsa, mini bagels and cream cheese, or round crackers and spray cheese

Steps: Spread the liquid ingredient on the round ingredient to make an edible target.

B. SERVE: ROUNDS

Serve butter cookies with a hole in the middle, mini-bagels, Oreos—any round cookie or cracker that can represent a target.

Cross, Circle, and Arrow Patterns

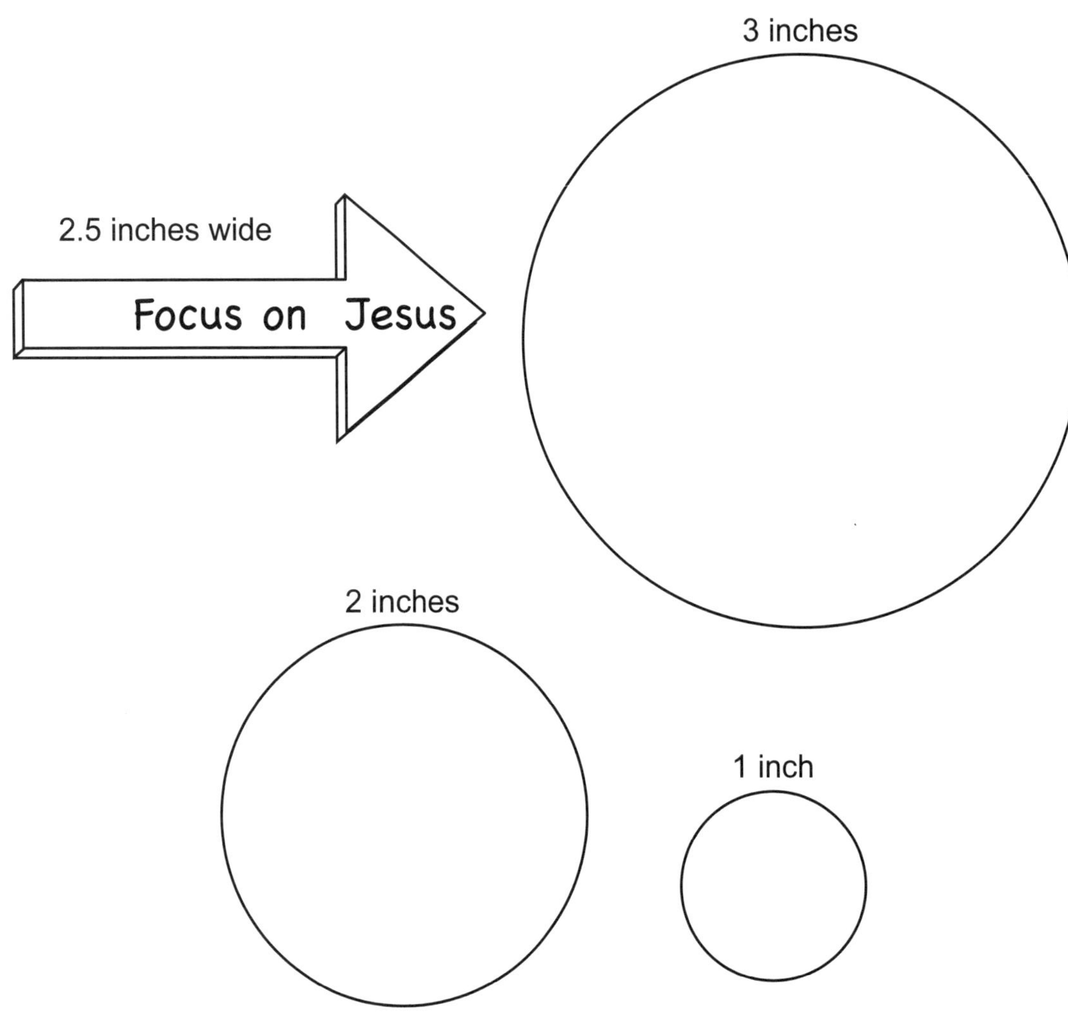

Session 3: Gymnastics
Key Word: Balance
Session Focus: Let us stand firm on God's Word!
Session Verses: Proverbs 4:25-27

Session Materials:

LET YOUR EYES LOOK STRAIGHT AHEAD, FIX YOUR GAZE DIRECTLY BEFORE YOU. MAKE LEVEL PATHS FOR YOUR FEET AND TAKE ONLY WAYS THAT ARE FIRM. DO NOT SWERVE TO THE RIGHT OR THE LEFT; KEEP YOUR FOOT FROM EVIL.—PROVERBS 4:25–27

Warm-Ups

- ❑ Stretch A: cards from commercial games
- ❑ Stretch B: Popsicle sticks
- ❑ Stretch C: Jenga or similar type stacking game

Get Ready! (Worship Arts)

- ❑ Processional: torch, Bible, carpenter's level, banner/flag with *BALANCE* on it in green letters
- ❑ Memory Verse Mania: pictures of motions or power point with words (optional)
- ❑ Joe Athlete Skit: green ring (tape, if sticking to wall)
- ❑ Bible Lesson: various sizes of rocks, packing peanuts or foam, long rope, 2-by-4 piece of wood with *God's Word* written on it; carpenter's level from processional

Get Set!

Games (Choose one of the following; instructions at end of session)

- ❑ Game A (Speed Stacking): large plastic cups, stopwatch or clock with second hand
- ❑ Game B (Balance Beams): chalk or masking tape, two 2-by-4 pieces of wood, cement blocks or large, sturdy buckets
- ❑ Game C (Egg Relay): several dozen eggs (real or plastic), spoons, chairs or cones

Crafts (Choose one of the following; instructions at end of session)

- ❑ Craft A (Ribbon Sticks): Popsicle sticks, crepe paper or ribbon in various colors, hot glue gun and glue sticks (adult use only) or quick-drying craft glue
- ❑ Craft B (Baby Balance Beams): small rectangle pieces of wood or tongue depressors, markers, stickers

Snacks (Choose one of the following; instructions at end of session)

- ❑ Snack Option A (Super Snack Stacks): rectangular crackers, cheese
- ❑ Snack Option B (Graham Crackers): graham crackers

Go!

Pictures/words of negative and positive actions from the Resource Section

Crossing the Finish Line!

2-by-4 balance beam with *God's Word* (from Bible Lesson)

Coach's Corner

Have you ever broken your leg or sprained an ankle? Even if you haven't experienced such physical trauma, you probably know what it is like to be out of balance. Being physically out of balance paints a vivid picture of what happens to us internally when we are spiritually off-kilter. Maybe we have spent too many hours at the office and not enough at home, or we have worked so hard at being a good parent that we have neglected to take time with the Lord. We have all been through times in our lives when our spiritual walk has been unsteady. Perhaps you are in the middle of such an experience right now. Take time to level things out in your heart. Find equilibrium with the Lord.

May this session encourage you to stand firm with the Lord—to look straight ahead, find only level paths for your feet, and keep your feet from evil. The Lord's richest blessings upon you and your students as you seek to find balance in God and God's Word!

Warm-Ups

SOME OF THE JOBS CAN BE COMBINED OR EXPANDED IF NECESSARY. (FOR INSTANCE, ONE PERSON CAN CARRY THE BIBLE AND THE TORCH; TWO PEOPLE COULD READ THE SCRIPTURE.)

1. Remember to find worship arts helpers during this time: torch bearer, Bible carrier, someone to bring in the BALANCE banner, someone to carry in the green ring, a child to carry in the carpenter's level, an older learner to read scripture.
2. Choose a Stretching Exercise from the end of the session to get ready for the session.

Transition to Worship Arts

When the Warm-Ups have concluded, ask the learners to help clean up if necessary. When you are ready to begin worship arts, give the quiet signal you have selected (See Overview of the Unit, Transition Quiet Symbol) and wait for the children's attention. Remind the learners to give their best respect to God during worship arts.

REMEMBER TO GET YOUR WORSHIP ARTS ASSISTANTS READY AT THE BACK OF THE ROOM.

Say, **As you walk to worship arts today, put one foot directly in front of the other.** (The heel of the right foot should touch the toes of the left foot and vice versa).

On Your Mark!

Recite the echo prayer (see Overview of the Unit), with a leader saying a word or phrase and the children repeating.

Get Ready! (Worship Arts)

1. Ready Rap!—After praying, recite the "Ready Rap!" (See Overview of the Unit.) Remind the students to show God their very best respect.
2. Processional—Play your chosen unit theme song and motion for the torch and the Bible to be brought forward and placed at the front. Next, motion for the carpenter's level to be brought to the front; finally the flag/banner should be brought to the front.
3. Singing—Prior to the session, choose four or five songs from your prearranged song list and then decide in which order to sing the songs. Put your CDs in order or arrange time to practice with your musicians. Either way, be sure to invite some older learners to help lead the singing and motions. Suggested Songs for this session: "Solid Rock," "Every Move I Make," "Step by Step," "In the Secret."
4. Memory Verse Mania—Recite the unit memory verses with motions. (See Overview of the Unit.) Conduct a contest between boys and girls to see who can say the verse the loudest and strongest!
5. Introduction of Theme and Sharing of Scripture—Use the skit, if possible, to emphasize the theme. If not possible, use the other option.

WITH JOE ATHLETE

[Joe Athlete enters the worship area doing (or attempting) somersaults, cartwheels, rolling, toe-touches, and so on. When he reaches the front, he stands on one foot for a long time. He puts his arms out to the sides. Give time for children to question what he is doing.]

Joe Athlete *[shouts out]*: Do you want to know what I am doing?

Worship arts leader: Yes, Joe, we'd all like to know what you're doing.

Joe: I am getting balance in my life! You know, like the gymnasts do. They have to make all kinds of moves and stay balanced.

[Joe shows the children that he is steady and can stand firm. He might invite someone else to come up and try what he is doing.]

Worship arts leader: That's great, Joe. You're keeping your body balanced. But there's another kind of balance we need in our lives.

Joe: There is?

Worship arts leader: Yes, and we're going to learn about that today. The Bible talks about standing firm and having balance.

Joe: All right. I sure want to find out about that. *[Joe hops out of the room on one foot.]*

[Call for a volunteer to bring up the green ring and link it to the black and red rings. Invite the student reading the scripture to come to the front to read Proverbs 4:25–27. After the scripture is read, pray together before beginning the Bible lesson.]

WITHOUT JOE ATHLETE

- If you cannot have Joe Athlete, the worship arts leader will invite the children to stand on one leg and balance for a minute or two, while calling for a volunteer to bring up the green ring and link it to the black and red rings.
- Then the volunteer or worship arts leader will point to the flag/banner and state, "Our theme word today is *BALANCE*. We will be talking about what it means to be steady with the Savior and we will learn how to stand firm on God's Word."
- Call up the child with the assignment to read the scripture. That volunteer will say, "The Bible talks about having balance and standing firm." Then he or she will read Proverbs 4:25–27 from the open Bible brought up during the processional.
- Ask a volunteer to pray that God would help you learn new things from the Bible. Be ready to begin the Bible lesson as soon as the prayer is finished.

6. Bible Lesson—The children will need their Bibles. You will want to gather rocks of different sizes, packing peanuts or foam, a long rope, a 2-by-4 piece of wood with *God's Word* written on it, and the carpenter's level from the processional.

   To prepare, make four different "lines" somewhere at the front of your worship arts area. Make one line out of the rocks and one line out of packing foam/peanuts; these lines should be relatively straight. Make a third line out of rope that curves from right to left. The fourth line should be a 2-by-4 piece of wood.

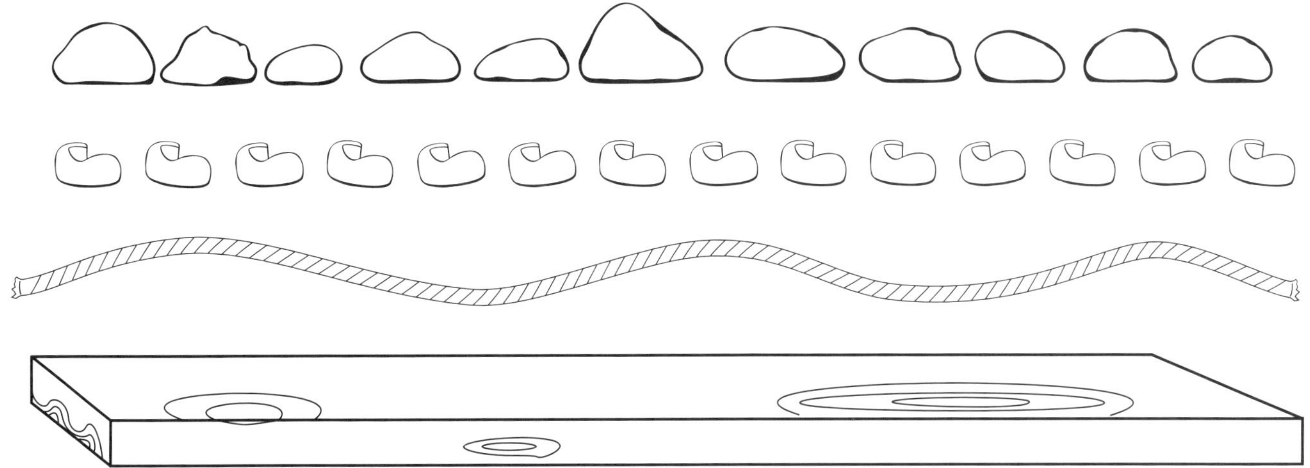

Introduce the Bible Lesson: Ask, **What was the theme of the first week?** Commitment, running, let us run God's race. **How would you put commitment to God in your own words?** Call on someone for a response. **What was the theme of our second session?** Focus, archery, we will fix our eyes on Jesus. **A testimony is a story we share about what God is doing in our lives. Do any of you want to share a story about how God has helped you have commitment or focus in your lives? Have you noticed any changes in your lives since you have had more commitment to God and fixed your eyes on Jesus?** Allow for short responses.

We are talking today about balance. Balance is also important in living for Jesus. Remember what the verses in Proverbs said about standing firm? Ask the children to share what they remember from the passage.

Find the scripture. Help the learners find the scripture in the Bible. Ask them if Proverbs is in the Old or New Testament. Tell them it comes right after the Book of Psalms. Ask the older learners to help the younger learners find the Book of Proverbs; then ask the younger learners to help the older learners find the big number 4 and the small numbers 25, 26, and 27.

Read and illustrate the scripture. Make sure everyone has his or her finger on the small 25, and then reread verse 25. Say, **Show me your eyes fixed straight ahead. Stare directly in front of you. Have we talked about where to fix our eyes?** Allow for response: on Jesus. **But I thought we were talking about balance? Do you think that focus and balance are related?** Allow for response. **It is hard to be in balance without focus and commitment. When our eyes are fixed on Jesus, we will be less distracted.** Ask the learners to look straight ahead again; go off to the side of the learners and do a crazy movement. **You did not even see me waving my arms and jumping around over here because your eyes were fixed ahead. If your eyes are fixed ahead of you—on Jesus—you will be less likely to wander over to the right or to the left.**

Then read verse 26 aloud. Ask, **What does the word *level* mean? Level means "flat, even, and equal."** Show the carpenter's level from the processional. **This tool is a level, and it helps me know when things are parallel to the ground and even. Levels are often used when hanging pictures or shelves on the wall to make sure the items are straight and balanced. When the bubble is between the lines, you know that the object is level and even.**

Tell the students you have some paths you want to walk and you want them to help you choose the right path. Say, **Verse 26 gives us guidelines for the right path. It says the path should be level and firm.** Go to the rock path and hit the rock. **Ouch. Do you think the rocks are firm?** Yes. Then place the level on the path (be sure it is on two unequal rocks). Ask for a child or two to come and look at the level. The path is *not* level. **This path is firm but not level, so it is not an okay path to take.** Next walk over to the path of packing peanuts. Place the level on the packing peanuts and bring up a few more witnesses. Try to get it as level as possible. Regardless of the level's reading, ask the volunteers to squeeze the foam pieces. Ask, **Is the path firm?** No. Move onto the next path. Quickly place the level on the rope and shout out, **It's pretty level!** Squeeze the rope with all your might and say, **It's definitely firm! It seems as if this path might be the right path to take. Can anyone think of a reason why I should not take this path?** Allow for responses.

Let's check the next verse. Read verse 27. **Raise your hands if you think the rope path swerves around.** All hands should be raised really high! **If my eyes are looking straight ahead and fixed before me on Jesus, do you think I could walk on this swerving path?** Let someone try to walk on the path and look ahead. **It will be very difficult to swerve right and left while staring straight ahead.**

Conclude the lesson. Move to the solid beam. Call on the children to witness that the beam is level and is the firmest of the four paths. Point out that the beam says *God's Word*. **Spending time in God's Word will balance us from the inside-out!** Walk across the beam looking straight ahead. Then say, **Anyone who wants to stand firm on God's Word—rise to your feet.**

Pray together. Use an echo prayer: Dear Jesus, *(echo)* thank you *(echo)* for giving us *(echo)* the Bible. *(echo)* Help us *(echo)* stay balanced *(echo)* in the Bible *(echo)* and in YOU. *(echo)* Amen.

7. Dismiss the learners by huddles and send groups directly to "Get Set!" Stations. If you are not rotating through stations, dismiss the learners by rows and send them to whichever activity they will complete first.

Get Set!

The learners will spend approximately 15 minutes in each station. If you are traveling from room to room, allow 12–13 minutes for the activity and 2–3 minutes to transition.

Station 1: Games

Choose one of the games from the end of the session. They all use aspects of physical balance to talk about spiritual balance.

Station 2: Crafts

Choose one of the crafts from the end of the session. Use the crafts to help reinforce the session and unit verses.

Station 3: Snacks

Choose one of the snacks from the end of the session. Remember to ask a child to pray before sharing in the snack!

As the children eat, tell some more of the story of Olympic hero Eric Liddell.

[Review the story thus far from weeks 1 and 2.]

Eric wasn't just a runner. Running wasn't all he did. He was studying and learning at the university. He was preparing to be a missionary to China, because he had felt that was what God wanted him to do. While he prepared, he continued to run races. But he had to keep balanced, because his commitment and focus were on God.

After his preparation, Eric Liddell did go to China. He went to the Anglo-Chinese College (more of an intermediate school to prepare for university) in Tientsin to teach. He continued to use his love of running as he taught boys in China. He taught them chemistry and sports. He began to hold weekly Bible studies for them in his home. Eric helped the boys have balance in their lives with physical, spiritual, and mental activities.

Go!

1. Gather all the learners together in one large group. Recite the "Ready Rap" (see Overview of the Unit) to get everyone refocused and transition to the closing portion of the session.
2. Keep Your Foot from Evil. You will need pictures and/or words of negative things (hitting, stealing, lying, smoking, and so on) and pictures/words of positive things (praying, Bible reading, worshiping, sharing, and so on). You might reproduce the words/pictures in the Resource Section as well as create your own.

   Scatter the pictures on the floor around the room. Depending on the size of your group, you may wish to visit each picture all together, send the children in pairs, or travel in small groups. As children approach each picture, they will choose whether to stand firm on that activity or keep their feet from that evil. Either way, literally stand on the picture or jump away.

YOU MAY WISH TO DIVIDE YOUR LEARNERS BY AGE FOR PRAYER TIME. LET THE OLDER LEARNERS PRAY IN THIS MANNER. GUIDE THE YOUNGEST LEARNERS (KINDERGARTEN AND YOUNGER) TO ANOTHER ROOM; INSTEAD OF PRAYING PRIVATELY, LET VOLUNTEERS PRAY ABOUT SPECIFIC WAYS TO STAND FIRM ON GOD'S WORD AND USE THE POSITIVE PICTURES AS PROMPTS TO THESE PRAYERS.

3. After all pictures have been viewed, ask the children to find their own individual space in the room—away from friends and distractions. Give each child several seconds to think of one way he or she needs to stand firm on God's Word. Then share a special prayer time together. Say, **We are going to pray together now. We will pray silently first. During this time, talk to God about ways to stand firm on him. This is not a time to talk to other people, just to God. Let's bow our heads, fold our hands, and close our eyes.**

Begin praying after a time of silence. **Dear God, we thank your for your Word. We want to stand firm on your promises.** Instruct the learners to pray, "Dear God, I want to commit to stand firm on your word by ________" and fill in the blank in their silent prayer to God. Allow them time to pray, but every few moments guide them further: **Ask God to help you in this new commitment.** (pause) **Ask God to show you new ways to stand firm on his Word.** (pause) **Now just enjoy waiting in silence.** (pause) **Ask God to help you when you start to swerve to the right or to the left.** (pause) **Ask God to forgive you for times you have not walked on a level path.** (pause)

Crossing the Finish Line!

1. Place in the exit doorway the 2-by-4 wooden beam that has *God's Word* written on it. The children can cross from the session into the "world" shouting, "I will stand firm on God's Word!"
2. Dismiss. Distribute any information sheets about the next session and follow the dismissal procedures for your church.

Resource Section

Stretching Exercises (Choose One)

Stretch A: Card Houses

Materials needed: cards from commercial games

Learners can build houses and towers out of cards. Encourage learners to build high, but with a firm base foundation.

Stretch B: Popsicle Stick Parade

Materials needed: Popsicle sticks

Write one to three words from the unit memory verses, Hebrews 12:1–2, on Popsicle sticks. Mix the sticks up and place them in a pile or a bag. If you have a large group you may want to make several sets.

Unscramble the verses by placing the sticks in the correct order, thus making a "Popsicle stick parade."

Stretch C: Jenga

Materials: Jenga game or similar type stacking game

Learners can play Jenga or a similar block-stacking game in groups of three or four.

Station 1: Games (Choose One)

A. Speed Stacks

Prep: Gather large plastic drinking cups, twelve cups per team.

Steps: Divide children into two teams. Each team will stack the cups in a 3-6-3 pattern. The 3-6-3 pattern has three stacks. The first and third stacks have three cups in each, two cups on the bottom and one cup stacked on top. The middle stack has six cups stacked, three on the bottom, two on the next level, and one on top. Give the teams some time to practice making these stacks and to delegate who will make which part of the pattern. Then have races to see who can complete the 3-6-3 pattern first. If you have time, let some of the children compete one-on-one.

IF YOU TYPE "SPEED STACKING" ON AN INTERNET SEARCH ENGINE, IT WILL BRING UP SEVERAL SITES ABOUT THIS SPORT. IF POSSIBLE, LET YOUR STUDENTS SEE VIDEO FOOTAGE FROM ACTUAL SPEED-STACKING TOURNAMENTS.

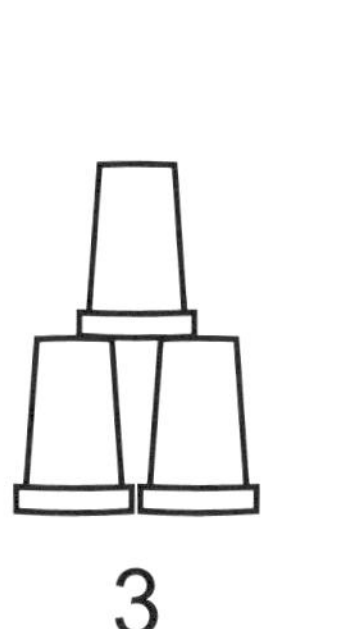

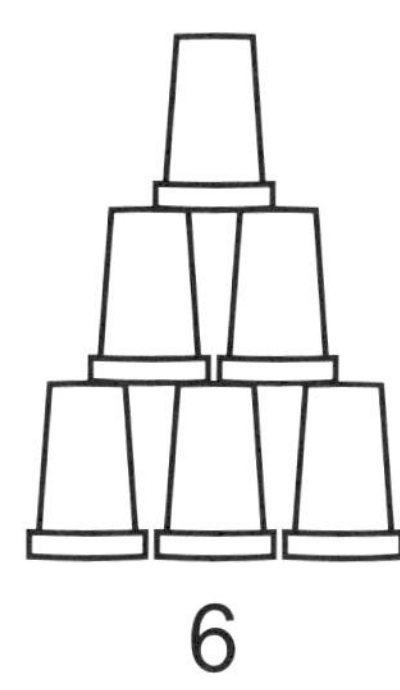

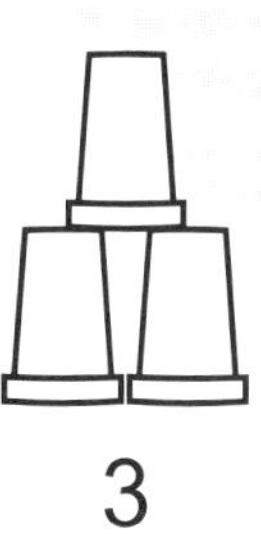

Spiritual Application: Ask the learners if they thought the task was hard or easy. Ask, **What happens when you put the cup too far on the right or on the left?** The cup slips down and won't be balanced. Point out that if the students practiced this activity for a long time, they would be able to do it much faster without any trouble. See if the students can find any connection with this statement and God. Reiterate that once we stand firm with Jesus, it becomes easier to stay balanced and make the right choices. When we stand firm on God's Word, we are less likely to swerve to the right and say something mean or swerve to the left and cheat on a test.

B. BALANCE BEAMS

Prep: Use two 2-by-4 pieces of wood, the one used in the Bible lesson and another. You will need concrete bricks or sturdy buckets, chalk, and a pool noodle or a yardstick. Draw a balance beam on the ground (chalk comes up easily from most carpets); set one 2-by-4 directly on the ground; set another 2-by-4 on sturdy concrete blocks or overturned buckets, about six to eight inches above ground.

REMEMBER THAT SAFETY IS OF UTMOST IMPORTANCE IN THIS ACTIVITY! ENCOURAGE THE OLDER LEARNERS TO HELP YOUNGER CHILDREN WALK ACROSS THE BEAMS.

Steps: Let students take turns walking across the three beams. Cross the beams, lowest to highest. Encourage the learners to look ahead. It will be hard for the learners not to look down at the beams. For an even greater challenge, walk across the beams with a pool noodle or yardstick in hands.

Spiritual Application: Read Proverbs 4:25–27. Ask three learners to each share how they followed these verses as they walked the beams.

C. EGG RELAY

Prep: Provide several dozen hard-boiled eggs (plastic if indoors), spoons, chairs or cones.

IF USING HARD-BOILED EGGS, KEEP REFRIGERATED BEFORE AND AFTER THE GAME SO THAT THEY CAN STILL BE EATEN LATER. REMEMBER GOOD STEWARDSHIP.

Steps: Divide the group into two teams (if uneven, one player on the smaller team will have to play twice). Explain that each person on the team will have a turn to hold the spoon with the egg on it, look straight ahead, and walk from the starting line down around the chair and back. This game is not about speed. The point of the game is to break (or drop) the fewest eggs. The teams will want to try to get all the members down and back with the same egg. If the egg falls, the player who dropped it will have to start over.

Spiritual Application: Review Proverbs 4:25–27. To keep the egg on the spoon the learners had to be deliberate, slow, and steady. They couldn't move quickly or turn their hands to the right or the left. The children will probably find incredible insights that never crossed your mind!

Station 2: Crafts (Choose One)

THIS CRAFT WORKS BEST WHEN THE RIBBON OR CREPE PAPER IS GLUED BY AN ADULT WITH A HOT GLUE GUN. IF YOU ARE NOT COMFORTABLE WITH GLUE GUNS, USING SCHOOL OR CRAFT GLUE WILL WORK BUT TAKE LONGER TO DRY. USE A PAPER CLIP TO REINFORCE THE GLUED PART. ALSO, DEPENDING ON THE SIZE OF YOUR GROUP, YOU MAY WISH TO PRECUT RIBBONS PRIOR TO THE SESSION.

A. Ribbon Sticks

Supplies: Popsicle sticks, crepe paper or one-inch ribbon in different colors, hot glue guns and sticks or fast-drying craft glue

Steps: Give each child two Popsicle sticks. All learners will need to cut two pieces of ribbon or crepe paper, each two to three feet in length. Fold each ribbon in half lengthwise, so you have two 1- to 1 1/2-foot lengths. Glue the center of the ribbon (where the fold is) on the end of the stick. Once dry, wave the ribbons in the air and around the room and recite memory verses from *God's Olympics*. For added fun, speak in a high voice when the ribbon is waving high; speak in a low voice when the ribbon is waving low.

TONGUE DEPRESSORS ARE A GOOD SUBSTITUTE FOR WOOD PIECES IN THIS ACTIVITY.

B. Baby Balance Beams

Supplies: Small, rectangular pieces of wood, permanent markers, stickers

Steps: Give each child a piece of wood. Write the word *Balance* on one side and *Proverbs 4:25–27* on the other. Decorate the balance beam with markers and stickers.

BALANCE

PROVERBS 4:25-27

Station 3: Snacks (Choose One)

A. Make: Super Snack Stacks

Ingredients: Rectangular crackers, cheese (small slices or spread), plates

The learners will stack the crackers and cheese in alternate layers, making the stack as high as possible without the stack falling off the plate.

B. Serve: Graham Crackers

Break graham crackers in half along the longer portion of the cracker to look like balance beams. Or, allow learners to stack crackers as high as possible before eating.

GOO BAR
GOO BAR
GOO BAR
HITTING
STEALING
LYING
SMOKING
PRAYING
BIBLE READING
WORSHIPING
SHARING

Session 4: Weight Lifting

Key Word: Strength

Session Focus: Let us Trust God for Strength!

Session Verse: Philippians 4:13

I can do everything through [Christ] who gives me strength.—Philippians 4:13

Session Materials:

Warm-Ups (Choose one of the following)

- ❑ Stretch A (Shakers): empty water bottles; craft beads; confetti or glitter
- ❑ Stretch B (Mini Weight Room): jump ropes, hula hoops, lightweight hand weights, small trampoline, and so on
- ❑ Stretch C (Resistance Push): none

Get Ready! (Worship Arts)

- ❑ Processional: torch, Bible, banner/flag with the word *STRENGTH* in yellow letters, big silver coffee can with new label (*GOD CAN*)
- ❑ Memory Verse Mania: words and pictures on a power point display (optional)
- ❑ Joe Athlete Skit: hand weights, the yellow ring (tape if sticking to wall)
- ❑ Bible Lesson: Bibles, large silver coffee can (from processional)

Get Set!

GAMES (CHOOSE ONE OF THE FOLLOWING; INSTRUCTIONS AT END OF SESSION)

- ❑ Game A (Watermelon Weight Lifting): CD, CD player, watermelons
- ❑ Game B (Three-Legged Race): bandannas or fabric to tie legs together
- ❑ Game C (Wait for the Lord): Bible, cones (optional)

CRAFTS (CHOOSE ONE OF THE FOLLOWING; INSTRUCTIONS AT END OF SESSION)

- ❑ Craft A (God CAN! Cans): coffee cans, paper to wrap around the cans, markers, stickers, tape
- ❑ Craft B (Hand Weight Hangings): various lightweight hand weights, paper plates, large sheets of heavy paper, washable paint of various colors
- ❑ Craft C (Dumbbells): toilet paper tubes, four-inch strips of paper, four-inch paper circles, mailing labels with session verse, stapler, tape

SNACKS (CHOOSE ONE OF THE FOLLOWING; INSTRUCTIONS AT END OF SESSION)

- ❑ Snack A (Donut Dumbbells): large pretzel rods, donut holes (large marshmallows can work in place of donut holes)
- ❑ Snack B (Power Bars): cereal or granola bars

Go!

God CAN! cans from Craft A or a coffee can covered in paper that says GOD CAN!, pieces of paper and pencils

Crossing the Finish Line!

Bible

Coaches' Corner

We all have times when we feel our strength is almost gone. We face these times physically and we may face these times spiritually. Sometimes we need to be reminded where to go for our strength.

Read Philippians 4:13; Isaiah 40:29–31; and Psalm 28:7. Find some time this week to truly be still and wait upon the Lord! Be a testimony to your students this week. How will you trust God for strength?

Warm-Ups

1. Remember to find worship arts helpers during this time: torch bearer, Bible carrier, someone to bring in the banner with STRENGTH written on it, someone to carry in the yellow ring, a child to carry in the coffee can with GOD CAN! on it, an older learner to read the scripture.
2. Choose a Stretching Exercise from the Resource Section to get ready for the session.

Transition to Worship Arts

When the Warm-Ups have concluded, ask the learners to help clean up if necessary. When you are ready to begin worship arts, give the quiet signal you have selected (see Overview of the Unit, Transition Quiet Signal) and wait for the learners' attention. Remind them to give their best respect to God during worship arts. Flex your muscles all the way to worship arts today!

On Your Mark!

Recite the echo prayer (See Overview of the Unit), with a leader saying a word or phrase and students repeating.

REMEMBER TO GET YOUR WORSHIP ARTS ASSISTANTS READY AT THE BACK OF THE ROOM.

Get Ready! (Worship Arts)

1. Ready Rap!—Upon completion of the prayer, say the "Ready Rap!" (See Overview of the Unit). Remind students to show God their very best respect.
2. Processional—Play your chosen unit theme song and motion for the torch and Bible to be brought forward and placed at the front. Motion the volunteer to bring to the front the large, silver can with *GOD CAN* written on it. Finally, motion to the volunteer carrying the flag/banner with the word *STRENGTH* written on it to come forward.
3. Singing—Prior to the session, choose four to five songs from your prearranged song list and then decide in which order to sing the songs. Put your CDs in order or arrange time to practice with your musicians. Either way, be sure to invite some older learners to help lead the singing and motions. Suggested songs for this session: "Every Move I Make," "Step by Step," "In the Secret," "Solid Rock," "I Get Down."
4. Memory Verse Mania—Recite the unit memory verses with motions (see Unit Introduction). Conduct a contest between sides of the room to see who can say the verses the strongest! Who can say the verses the fastest? Invite volunteers to say the verses alone!
5. Introduction of Theme and Sharing of Scripture—Use the skit, if possible, to get at the theme. If not possible, use the other option.

WITH JOE ATHLETE

[Joe enters lifting weights and continues pumping and flexing his way to the center of the stage]

Worship arts leader: Hey, Joe. That looks like hard work.

Joe: It sure is. Betcha can't guess what sport we're talking about today! *[allows for response]* I'm working on becoming one of those guys who can lift tons of weight. I'm building up my strength. See how strong I'm getting? *[flexes muscles]*

Worship arts leader: Oh, sure, Joe. Really strong.

Joe: Guess where I get my strength!

Worship arts leader: What do you think, kids?

Joe *[after the kids respond]***:** I'll give you a hint! *[pulls a can from his pocket that says SPINACH]*

Worship arts leader *[taking can and showing it to the learners]***:** You get your strength from spinach, Joe?

Joe: I knew you would probably think that I'm like Popeye and get my strength from spinach. But that's not true! The hint is the *can*! Today we are talking about how we *can* have strength!

Worship arts leader: That's right, Joe. Let's read something from the Bible that talks about strength.

[Invite a volunteer to bring up the yellow ring and attach it to the other three rings. Another volunteer will read Philippians 4:13 while another holds up the GOD CAN can. Pray. Joe leaves the stage lifting weights. The Bible lesson begins after the prayer concludes.]

WITHOUT JOE ATHLETE

- If you cannot have Joe Athlete, the worship arts leader will bring up to the stage with him or her some very light hand weights. Ask for volunteers to come up and show everyone how to use the weights.
- Ask the other children to answer some questions: **What sport do you think we are looking at today?** Allow for responses. **What do you need to be able to do weight lifting as a sport?** Some may say practice or big muscles, but what we are looking for here is the word *strength*. Ask your volunteers who are still pumping weights, **Do you think getting strong is easy? How hard was it to lift those weights? What about some that were heavier?** Wait for responses.
- Call up your volunteer with the yellow ring and let him or her add it to the other three rings. Then he or she will point out the flag/banner and state, "Our theme word today is STRENGTH. We will be talking about where we can turn when we feel weak."
- Call up another volunteer to read Philippians 4:13 while someone else holds up the GOD CAN can. Pray together.
- Be ready to begin the Bible lesson as soon as the prayer is finished.

6. Bible Lesson—The children will need their Bibles. Bring out the large silver coffee can with the label *GOD CAN*! (from processional).

   Introduce the Bible lesson. Ask the learners to fill in the blanks: I CAN do (everything) through (Christ) who gives me (strength). Affirm that yes, God is able to do anything. Say, **God can give us strength in all circumstances. The strength God gives is sometimes physical. We might be sick and he touches our bodies to make us well; we might be really tired at school, and we ask God to give us strength to get through the day. But God also gives us strength in our minds and our hearts. Think of a time that was difficult in your lives: maybe a friend moved away, a grandma was sick, a brother was in the hospital, or someone died. God also gives strength to us during those times.**

   Find the scripture. Ask the children to open their Bibles to the center pages. Explain that they should be in the Old Testament in the Book of Psalms. Give the students a few moments to all get to the right book. Then instruct them to find chapter 28, which is the big number, and verse 7, which is the smaller number.

   Read and explain the scripture. Once all the children have found the passage, read the verse together. Say, **Right now we are going to study this verse and make sure we understand what it means.** Pick apart the scripture line by line. Read the first phrase: "The LORD is my strength and my shield." **Who will describe what *strength* means, in your own words?** Not being tired, feeling healthy, being encouraged and not disappointed. **What does a shield do?** It protects. **So, God helps us and protects us. The Bible is true. We can believe that God can give us strength.**

Look at the next line, "my heart trusts in him, and I am helped." Ask, **How can we learn to trust in God?** Pray, not be afraid, take courage, read verses in the Bible about God being our helper and strength, remember times God has helped us in the past. **What happens when we trust God?** Verse 7 states, "I am helped."

Finally, look at the last half of the verse: "My heart leaps for joy and I will give thanks to him in song." **What does it mean when your heart leaps for joy? You are excited; people who leap have strength and are not tired. People who leap are full of good stuff, and this verse explains that the good stuff is the joy of the Lord.** Allow the children to leap around the room as you count on your fingers to 10. When you reach number 10, the children should freeze; instruct them to return to their seats.

Conclude the lesson. **The verse also says that we should "give thanks to him in song."** Sing a few songs to conclude the Bible lesson. Suggested songs for this time include "I've got the Joy, Joy, Joy, Joy Down in My Heart" (traditional); "The Joy of the Lord Is My Strength" with all the verses; and "Joy" (*Every Move I Make* CD).

Pray together. When the singing is finished, ask for a child to pray first. Then say an echo prayer together: Dear Jesus, (*echo*) thank you (*echo*) for giving me (*echo*) strength. (*echo*) Please help me (*echo*) trust you (*echo*) in everything. (*echo*) Amen.

7. Dismiss the learners by huddles and send groups directly to "Get Set!" stations. If you are not rotating through stations, dismiss the children by rows and send them to whichever activity they will complete first.

Get Set!

The learners will spend approximately 15 minutes in each station. If you are traveling from room to room, allow 12–13 minutes for the activity and 2–3 minutes to transition.

STATION 1: GAMES

Choose a game from the end of the session. Each of the games illustrates an aspect of strength.

STATION 2: CRAFTS

Choose a craft from the end of the session to reinforce the session verse, Philippians 4:13.

STATION 3: SNACKS

Choose one of the snacks from the end of the session. Invite volunteers to pray aloud, thanking the Lord for the snack and all God's many blessings.

As the children eat, tell some more of the story of Olympic hero Eric Liddell.

[Review the story thus far from weeks 1, 2, and 3]

Eric married, and he and his family continued as missionaries in China. He was still serving as a missionary when World War II broke out. His wife and children left the country to be safe. But Eric stayed behind to keep working for God in China. When the Japanese invaded the place where he was, he and other missionaries were confined to a certain area. But then the Japanese ordered them to a prison camp in another place. They went by train. There were electric fences around them. There was never enough food. But God's strength was with Eric.

Eric took on many responsibilities to help the other prisoners in the camp. He was able to help by teaching the children in the camp, by preaching in camp services, and by being a peacemaker. Though the children were always hungry, he was able to help them get excited about sports. Eric had a commitment and focus on God. He had God's strength to run God's race.

Go!

1. Gather all the learners together in one large group. They should bring their "God CAN cans" from Craft A if you used that option. Or, bring over the covered coffee can used at the beginning of the session. Recite the "Ready Rap" to get everyone refocused and transition to the closing portion of the session.
2. Give the children pieces of paper and pencils. Explain, **God can give us strength in any situation. Write down or draw any prayer requests or burdens that are heavy in your lives. Then put those heavy burdens in the God CAN! Cans.** The children will put the papers in their own personal cans or in the group can.
3. Pray over each of these requests and encourage your students to believe that God can and will give us strength. You may even wish to pass the can(s) around the circle and allow the children to pray a silent prayer over each can (without reading the paper inside). When you are finished, ask the learners if any of them feel better about the burden they put in the can(s). **Even if we don't feel better right now, we will keep praying for God to bring strength. We can trust God that he can and will give strength in all circumstances.**

Crossing the Finish Line!

If you are using the water activities in the next session, consider inviting the children to wear their swimsuits and bring towels.

1. Read Psalm 28:7 again to the learners.
2. Ask for volunteers to share ways that God has given them strength in the past. After each person shares, instruct all to leap in the air and shout, "Thank you, God, for giving __________ strength!" (Say the child's name.) Continue as times allows.
3. As the children leave the room, encourage them to leap through the doorway shouting, "I can do everything through [Christ] who gives me strength!"
4. Distribute any information sheets for the next session and follow the dismissal procedures for your church.

Resource Section

Stretching Exercises

Stretch A: Shakers

Materials needed: Empty water bottles; craft beads; confetti or glitter

Remove labels from empty bottles. Fill containers with beads and confetti. Instruct the children to write their names on the bottles and save the shakers for worship arts.

Stretch B: Mini Weight Room

Materials needed: Jump ropes, hula hoops, lightweight hand weights, a small trampoline, and so on

Set up a mini weight room with jump ropes, hand weights (5 lbs. or less), hula hoops, and a small trampoline. Learners can play independently with the items or travel to each item in a "circuit."

Stretch C: Resistance Push

Materials needed: None

Pair learners as partners. One partner lies down on his or her back and puts legs up in the air. The other person stands by the raised feet of the partner and tries to gently push the partner's legs down to the ground. The partner lying down tries to keep his or her legs in the air. Be certain to point out to each set of partners that part of gaining strength is experiencing resistance.

Station 1: Games (Choose One)

A. Watermelon Weight Lifting

Prep: Provide a CD, a CD player, and a watermelon or two.

Steps: This game is played just like Hot Potato, substituting a watermelon for a potato. Ask learners to sit in a circle. Assign a volunteer to stop and start the music. When the music begins, the children pass the watermelon around the circle. When the music stops, whoever is holding the watermelon is out of the game. Start a second circle that plays simultaneously for those learners who are "out" to stay occupied while the others finish the game. (No one gets "out" in this second circle.)

Spiritual Application: Ask the learners to describe how it felt to lift the heavy watermelon. It was hard, discouraging, frustrating; I felt as if it couldn't be done, I wanted to quit, I had to roll it on the ground, I was afraid I was going to drop it. Remind the students that when those feelings happen, we need to trust God for strength.

Variation: You may opt to use a cantaloupe or honeydew melon instead of a watermelon.

B. THREE-LEGGED RACE

Prep: Supply bandannas or fabric to tie legs together.

Steps: Pair up the children. (If there is an odd number of children, a leader can be a partner.) They should stand shoulder to shoulder with their partners. Leaders will tie the right leg of one learner to the left leg of the other (the inner legs of the duo). All partners will race at the same time to see who crosses the finish line first. If a pair falls over, they have to stand up and try again from the place they fell.

Spiritual Application: Encourage the students to express what this experience taught them individually about God. You may wish to point out that building strength doesn't happen quickly; you have to walk with the Lord and be in step with him. Also, you may fall or trip in your walk. Having strength means you stand up and keep on going forward!

C. WAIT FOR THE LORD

Prep: Provide a Bible and cones or small trash cans.

Steps: Instruct the children to do twenty jumping jacks, then immediately run five times around a path designated with several cones (or in place for thirty seconds), then immediately spin around ten times, then immediately do fifteen toe touches. (If the children are not out of breath, give them a few more physical activities to complete.) Afterwards, allow the learners the chance to sit down.

Spiritual Application: Ask the children how they feel. We hope their descriptions indicate being tired, out of breath, want to rest, need water, and so on. Explain that the best way to trust God for strength is to wait for him often. Then read from Isaiah 40:31: "Those who wait for the Lord shall renew their strength" (NRSV). Ask the learners what they think it means to wait for or upon the Lord. (The NIV uses the word "hope." There are many acceptable answers: praying before making decisions, sitting down every day to talk with God and read God's Word, being still and calm while thinking about God and listening to the silence, sharing prayer requests with others, quoting your favorite Bible verses. **Waiting for the Lord encourages us and truly does give strength.**

More Steps: Repeat the physical exercises done earlier. Do twenty jumping jacks; then sit down and read the Bible. Next run five laps or run in place for thirty seconds; then sit down and share favorite things about the Lord. Then spin around ten times and rest by being still and listening to the silence. Finally, do ten toe touches; then sit down to pray. Discuss how much easier it was to take breaks in between. We need to stop many times during the day to wait for the Lord. Challenge the learners to wait for the Lord every day in the next week. Pray over the children and ask God to help them know how to wait for him every day.

STATION 2: CRAFTS (CHOOSE ONE)

A. GOD CAN! CANS

Supplies: Coffee can or other aluminum can for each student (be sure none have a rough edge), paper to wrap around the cans, markers, stickers, tape

Steps: Wrap and tape paper around the coffee cans (or smaller cans). Write GOD CAN! on each paper. Decorate with markers, stickers, crayons, and so on. Write *Philippians 4:13* and the actual verse on the paper if you so choose. Explain to the learners that they will use these cans at the end of today's session.

B. HAND WEIGHT HANGINGS

Supplies: Various lightweight hand weights, paper plates, large sheets of heavy paper, washable paint of various colors

Steps: Put a different color of paint on each paper plate. (You may choose to use shoe box lids instead.) Put one or two hand weights on each plate. Dip the weights and stamp them on the paper or roll the weights to make tracks all over the page. Let the children paint their handprints on the pages as a commitment to trust God for strength. Write *Christ gives me strength* or a similar message somewhere on the sheets. You may choose to make a large banner for each class, taping the individual sheets together to display on the wall.

C. DUMBBELLS

Supplies: Toilet paper tubes, four-inch strips of paper, four-inch paper circles, mailing labels with session verse on it, stapler, tape

Steps: Each dumbbell needs one toilet paper tube, four strips of paper, two paper circles, and one mailing label with *Philippians 4:13* printed on it. Decide ahead of time if each child will make one or two dumbbells, and plan supplies accordingly. Instruct the learners to decorate one side of the paper circles and the outside of the toilet paper tubes. Tape or staple two strips of paper in each end of the tube, one across from the other and sticking out the end. Then fold the strips of paper over the edge of the tube outward. Tape or staple one circle on the strips at each end; be certain the decorated side faces outward. Add the mailing label somewhere on the dumbbell.

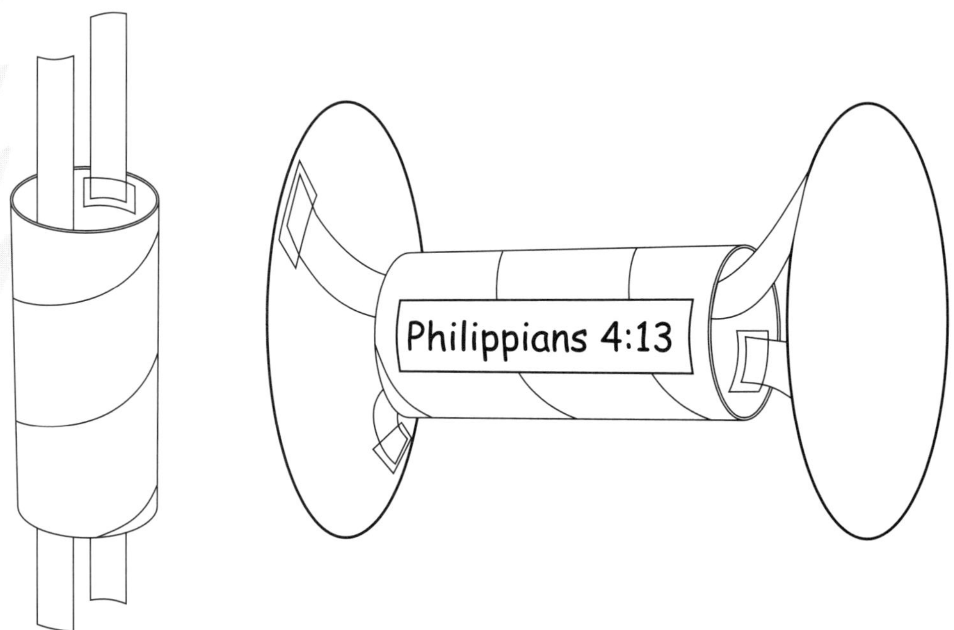

STATION 3: SNACKS (CHOOSE ONE)

A. MAKE: DONUT DUMBBELLS

Ingredients: Large pretzel rods, donut holes (large marshmallows can work in place of donut holes)

Steps: Give each learner a pretzel rod and four donut holes. Break each pretzel in half. Place one donut on each end of the pretzel rod and enjoy!

B. SERVE: POWER BARS

Offer the children cereal or granola bars to reinforce the idea of strength.

SESSION 5: SWIMMING

KEY WORD: ENDURANCE

SESSION FOCUS: LET US PRESS ON TOWARD THE GOAL!

SESSION VERSES: PHILIPPIANS 3:12–14

SESSION MATERIALS:

WARM-UPS (CHOOSE ONE OF THE FOLLOWING; INSTRUCTIONS AT END OF SESSION)

- ❏ Stretch A (Swimming in Place): chairs
- ❏ Stretch B (Noodle Knockout): foam pool noodles
- ❏ Stretch C (Rain Gutter Races): two new gutters, water, balloons, straws (optional)

GET READY! (WORSHIP ARTS)

- ❏ Processional: torch, Bible, kitchen colander (strainer), banner/flag with ENDURANCE written on it in blue letters
- ❏ Memory Verse Mania: various pool toys and beach gear (towels, goggles, flippers, snorkel tube, swimmies); small baby pool(s) without water
- ❏ Joe Athlete Skit: flippers, swimmies, towel, swim cap, float tube around waist, pool noodle in hand, goggles on head, blue ring (tape if sticking to wall)
- ❏ Bible Lesson: marbles or similar type item; colander from processional; water in a clear pitcher or bowl; food coloring; empty wading pool

I PRESS ON TO TAKE HOLD OF THAT FOR WHICH CHRIST JESUS TOOK HOLD OF ME. BROTHERS, I DO NOT CONSIDER MYSELF YET TO HAVE TAKEN HOLD OF IT. BUT ONE THING I DO: FORGETTING WHAT IS BEHIND AND STRAINING TOWARD WHAT IS AHEAD, I PRESS ON TOWARD THE GOAL TO WIN THE PRIZE FOR WHICH GOD HAS CALLED ME HEAVENWARD IN CHRIST JESUS.—PHILIPPIANS 3:12–14

GET SET!

GAMES (CHOOSE ONE OF THE FOLLOWING; INSTRUCTIONS AT END OF SESSION)

- ❏ Game A (Drip, Drip, Drop): pitcher and hose (or trashcan filled with water)
- ❏ Game B (Water Balloon Toss): water balloons in a tub
- ❏ Game C (Beach Obstacle Course): beach balls, hula hoops, kiddie pools, pool noodles, life jackets

CRAFTS (CHOOSE ONE OF THE FOLLOWING; INSTRUCTIONS AT END OF SESSION)

- ❏ Craft A (Life Jackets): brown paper grocery sacks (one for each child), orange paint and paintbrushes or markers, scissors, white ribbon (about one to two inches thick), mailing labels with session verses printed on them
- ❏ Craft B (Underwater Words): white crayons, white card stock or paper, blue watercolor paint, paintbrushes

SNACKS (CHOOSE ONE OF THE FOLLOWING; INSTRUCTIONS AT END OF SESSION)

- ❏ Snack A (Beach Towel Crackers): graham crackers, different colors of icing, plastic knives
- ❏ Snack B (Fishbowl): blue Jell-O and gummy fish in plastic cups
- ❏ Snack C (Goldfish and Lifesavers): goldfish crackers, LifeSavers candy

WATER IS USED TODAY, AND THE CHILDREN WOULD ENJOY WEARING THEIR SWIMSUITS FOR THIS SESSION. BRING TOWELS AND CLOTHES TO CHANGE INTO. CONSIDER OTHER ARRANGEMENTS NEEDED FOR ACCOMMODATING THE "WET" ACTIVITIES.

GO!

Video of a swimmer swimming laps (optional)

CROSSING THE FINISH LINE!

Sprinkler

Coaches' Corner

Read Philippians 3:12–14 over and over again. Read it every day this week and ask the Lord to give you a fresh experience with endurance. I hope the very words of those verses bring true encouragement to your heart. Seek the Lord and ask him to help you in "forgetting what is behind and straining toward what is ahead" (v 13). How do you personally need to press on toward your heavenly prize? Don't skim over that question. Allow the Lord to work in the secret places of your heart. Remember, God has called you in Christ Jesus. Take courage and push forth! Do you need endurance today? May you find all the perseverance you need in the Savior.

Warm-Ups

1. During this introduction time, choose four or five willing children to help with worship arts. Choose one person to carry in the torch, one person to carry in the open Bible, one person to carry in the kitchen colander or strainer, one person to carry in the blue ring, and one person to carry in the banner stating *ENDURANCE*. Remember to choose children of all ages. Remind the helpers that they will enter the room one at a time while the song plays. If you have enough space and volunteers to practice, go for it! If not, set up the students for success by positioning them in a location where they can see the worship arts leader and wait for his or her nod. Last, invite an older child to read scripture.
2. Choose a Stretching Exercise from the end of the session to get students ready for the session.

Transition to Worship Arts

When the Warm-Ups have concluded, ask the learners to help clean up if necessary. When you are ready to begin worship arts, give the quiet signal you have selected (see Overview of the Unit, Transition Quiet Signal) and wait for the children's attention. Remind learners to give their best respect to God during worship arts. Silently swim with your arms as you make your way to worship arts.

REMEMBER TO GET YOUR WORSHIP ARTS ASSISTANTS READY AT THE BACK OF THE ROOM.

On Your Mark!

Recite the echo prayer (see Overview of the Unit), with a leader saying a word or phrase and the students repeating.

Get Ready! (Worship Arts)

1. Ready Rap!—After the prayer is finished, call out the "Ready Rap!" (See Overview of the Unit.) Continue to focus the students by reminding them that we want to show God our very best respect.
2. Processional—Play your chosen unit theme song and motion for the torch and Bible to be brought forward and placed at the front. Then motion for the kitchen colander (strainer) to be brought to the front, and finally for the flag/banner to be brought up.
3. Singing—Start the singing portion of worship arts with Steven Curtis Chapman's song "Dive." Distribute pool noodles and beach balls for the children to toss and wave during this song. Several adults should stand among the crowd. Collect the props before continuing. Other songs could include "Solid Rock," "In the Secret," "Step by Step," "Every Move I Make," "I Get Down," and "Joy!"
4. Memory Verse Mania—Prepare various pool toys and beach gear (towels, goggles, flippers, snorkel tube, swimmies) with phrases of the unit memory verses (see Overview of the Unit) on them, one phrase per item. Place the items in random order inside a baby pool (without water). Prepare more than one pool of phrases if you have a large group.

   Children will arrange the items so that the phrases of the verse are in the correct order. If you have more than one pool, divide the learners in teams and race to see who can put the verse in order first. Once the verses are complete, say the verses together and do the motions from memory. (See Overview of the Unit.)
5. Introduction of Theme and Sharing of Scripture—Use the skit, if possible, to illustrate the theme. If not possible, use the other option.

WITH JOE ATHLETE:

Worship arts leader: Here comes our friend Joe. Hi, Joe.

[Joe waddles up the aisle in swimming attire: flippers, swimmies, towel, swim cap, float tube, pool noodle, goggles, and so on. He might sprinkle water from a squirt toy.]

Joe Athlete: Hi, everyone!

[When Joe gets to the front he sits down in the wading pool—not fitting and almost breaking the sides.]

Joe Athlete *[excitedly, looking at banner]***:** Today our theme is End-you-rance.

Worship arts leader: What did you say, Joe?

Joe Athlete *[looks at kids]***:** Isn't that what the banner says?

Worship arts leader *[waiting for children to respond]***:** No, Joe. Try again.

Joe Athlete: Oh, I get it. Our theme is "In-dewer-ants! Ants?! Like the bugs? Why are we talking about ants? Ick!"

Worship arts leader *[looking at children]***:** Kids, what's the word?

Joe Athlete *[saying it right finally]***:** Oh, endurance. Let's see. Having endurance means pressing on toward the goal. It means that you never give up! Commitment is agreeing to do something, and endurance is sticking to it through the end. Do you know what sport we're talking about today that takes a lot of endurance?

Worship arts leader *[after children have answered]***:** That's right. Swimming. In a race the swimmers have to swim a number of laps. It doesn't just take speed. It takes breathing right, making the turn properly, using the proper strokes. It takes forgetting what's behind you and pushing (or straining) forward. It takes keeping strong until the end. We're going to find out that endurance is also important to us as we follow Christ.

Joe Athlete: Okay. So I'm going to go practice my endurance. *[walks out with all his stuff still on him, waving his arms in a swimming stroke]*

[Call your volunteer with the blue ring to bring it to the front and link it with the other rings. Ask that volunteer or another to read the scripture passage, Philippians 3:12–14, from the open Bible. Ask another child or adult volunteer to pray. Be ready to begin the Bible lesson after the prayer.]

WITHOUT JOE ATHLETE:

- If you cannot have Joe Athlete, bring to the front the items mentioned in the skit. Ask a child or two to the front to look the items over. The worship leader will ask, **What are these things used for?** After the children have answered, ask, **What do you think is important in swimming?** Let the children respond. **We're going to look at one thing that is important for swimmers to have.**
- Invite your volunteer with the blue ring to bring it to the front. After linking it with the other rings, he or she should point to the flag with the word *ENDURANCE* on it. He or she says, "Today our theme is endurance. Having endurance means pressing on toward the goal. Having endurance also means that you never give up! Commitment is agreeing to do something, and endurance is sticking with it through to the end."
- Call on another volunteer to read Philippians 3:12–14 from the open Bible brought forward during the processional.
- Pray as soon as the passage is finished.

6. Bible Lesson—The children will need their Bibles. Set out the kitchen colander (strainer) from the processional. You will also need marbles, water in a clear pitcher or bowl, food coloring, and the empty wading pool used earlier.

   Introduce the Bible lesson. Show the kitchen colander. Ask the learners if they have ever seen one and if anyone knows what to do with it. **I am holding a colander, also known as a strainer. People use this kind of strainer when cooking spaghetti to get the noodles out of the hot water, or when cooking ground beef to get the grease off. I can also use a strainer to wash berries or rinse vegetables. When I use a strainer, the good stuff stays and the yucky stuff goes! What do you think this strainer can teach us about God? What can this strainer teach us about endurance?** Allow for responses. See if the children find any connection between the strainer and Philippians 3:12–14.

Find the scripture. Help the learners find Philippians in their Bibles by instructing them to open to the New Testament. Tell them, **It comes after Matthew, Mark, Luke, John, and Acts. It's one of the letters written by a missionary named Paul. Go past Romans, 1 and 2 Corinthians, Galatians, and Ephesians and you'll come to the Book of Philippians.** Older students can help the younger ones find the book. **Put your finger on the big number 3, then the smaller numbers 12, 13, and 14.**

Read and explain the scripture. Read the scripture verses together. **The scripture tells us to forget what is behind, to strain toward the goal ahead, and to press on toward the prize. What might stand in the way of running after Jesus or make us lose our focus or cause us to go down the wrong path and lose our balance or make us lose strength?** Call attention to the bowl of water. Drop a different shade of food coloring into the water for each obstacle named. **Now name different ways to press on toward the goal of being like Jesus.** With each response (pray, know God, read the Bible, share faith with others, serve, worship, memorize scripture, be still and listen to God, and so on) add a marble to the dirty water.

Reread the part of verse 13 that states, "forgetting what is behind and straining toward what is ahead." Explain, **Sometimes when we have obstacles in our lives, we may feel as if they are all around us. But God's Word teaches us to forget those things. How? By getting rid of them—pouring them out of our lives and into Jesus. The Bible also says to strain toward what is ahead, the goal. What's the goal?** Being like Jesus. **What's the prize?** Eternity with God!

Conclude the lesson. Ask, **What does a strainer do?** It leaves the good stuff and gets rid of the yucky stuff. Stand over an empty wading pool and hold the strainer up so all can see. Pour the dirty water and the marbles into the strainer. **What's left?** Show the children that only the marbles remain. Shake the strainer so drops of water continue to slowly drip out. **Forgetting the bad things and leaving them behind us can take a while, but it can be done! We won't literally strain our problems in a strainer, but God does want us to push on and press ahead by never giving up on our faith. Allow the children to respond about what the strainer and these verses have taught them.**

Pray together. Use an echo prayer: Dear Jesus, *(echo)* thank you *(echo)* for teaching us *(echo)* about endurance. *(echo)* Help us *(echo)* forget what is behind *(echo)* and strain toward the goal. *(echo)* Help us *(echo)* to press on *(echo)* toward the prize. *(echo)* Amen.

7. Dismiss the learners by huddles and send groups directly to "Get Set!" Stations. If you are not rotating through stations, dismiss the learners by rows and send them to whichever activity they will complete first.

Get Set!

The learners will spend approximately 15 minutes in each station. If you are traveling from room to room, allow 12-13 minutes for the activity and 2-3 minutes to transition.

TWO OF THESE GAMES WILL CAUSE THE STUDENTS TO GET WET; SWIMWEAR WOULD BE THE IDEAL ATTIRE, AND OUTDOORS WOULD BE THE APPROPRIATE PLACE. YOUR SITUATION, HOWEVER, MAY CALL FOR YOU TO USE THE VARIATIONS AND PROVIDE PROTECTIVE COVERING FOR THE CHILDREN.

Station 1: Games

Choose one of the games from the end of the session as the children think about endurance.

Station 2: Crafts

Choose a craft from the end of the session to reinforce the session verses and concepts learned during *God's Olympics.*

Station 3: Snacks

Choose a snack from the end of the session. Invite a child to thank God for the food before serving and eating.

As the learners eat, finish telling the story of Olympic hero Eric Liddell.

[Review the story thus far from sessions 1, 2, 3, and 4]

While in the prison camp, Eric could be found getting water, taking out the garbage, and cleaning up as well as helping children with their studies. He used what he could find to make balls and sticks for playing sports. He led Bible studies. He helped people get along with one another. He spent quiet time with God in the mornings.

Time kept on going by. Eric had been in the prison camp for eighteen months. Then the people in charge cut the food rations to the camp. Prisoners started getting sick. Eric began to feel unwell. He had bad headaches, and they grew worse. Before the war was over, Eric died in the camp. But he had run the race. He had endured to the end. And he had won the prize.

GO!

1. Upon completing the three stations, learners should all come together in one large group. Recite the "Ready Rap" to get everyone refocused and transition to the closing portion of the session.

2. "Turnaround" Talk. Show a video of a swimmer in slow motion if possible. If not, ask the children to think about a swimming race they have seen. Focus on what happens at the end of the lane. The swimmer turns around. **In swimming, focus and balance are important. So is strength. Good breathing and the right body shape matter. But in a race, when pressing on toward the goal, "turnarounds" are very important!**

   Ask, **How are "turnarounds" in swimming like our Christian faith and the race we are running for Jesus?** Allow for responses. **Turning around is like asking for forgiveness and getting back on the right path. Remember, in our gymnastics session we talked about level paths. Philippians 3:13 tells us to forget what is behind and strain toward what is ahead.** Ask the children to think about whether there is anything in their lives they want to turn away from and leave behind.

3. Personal Prayer time. Instruct the students to find their own places to stand three to five feet in front of a wall. Tell the children that this prayer time is between them and the Lord. Explain, **The first part of the prayer time will involve asking for forgiveness for anything in your life you wish to leave behind.** Give some ideas, such as talking back to parents, being mean to siblings, talking behind friends' backs, lying, cheating, and so on. **If you can't think of any sin in your life, ask God to help you think of something you need to turn away from—maybe a bad habit such as watching too much TV or playing video games too long every day.**

   Next say, **The second step in the prayer is to physically walk to the wall and press on it very hard. While you are pressing on the wall, ask God to help you press on toward the goal of being like Jesus! Trust God for endurance and ask him to help you never to give up in your Christian faith. When you are finished, turn around and face the other way. Thank and praise God for your time at *God's Olympics*. Tell God your favorite things and ask God to help you remember this special time.**

   Demonstrate an example of this prayer and pray out loud. Remind the students that they will pray silently. Enjoy watching your students on this "turnaround" prayer, and pray for the commitments they are making.

   When the students are finished, tell them, **The next time you are in a hard situation or having a difficult time, go stand against the wall and push hard while you pray. It will be a reminder that God can give strength and endurance!**

   Variation: Send younger learners to the hallway with an adult. Instruct them to simply push hard on a wall, and let children take turns praying for anything they choose. Then pray the following echo prayer: Dear Jesus, *(echo)* please help me *(echo)* never to give up *(echo)* living for you. *(echo)* Amen. *(echo)*

Crossing the Finish Line!

1. If the students wore their swimsuits or clothes that can get wet, take the finish line outdoors and set up a sprinkler. Run through the sprinkler one at a time. As each child runs through, he or she shouts, "Let us press on toward the goal!"

   If the students did not wear swimsuits, use a spray mist bottle or bathroom squirt toy to sprinkle the children with water as they go through the doorway. Each one should shout, "Let us press on toward the goal!"

2. Distribute the information sheets about any closing ceremony activity and dismiss the children according to your church procedures.

Resource Section

Stretching Exercises (Choose One)

STRETCH A: SWIMMING IN PLACE

Materials needed: Chairs

Learners will take turns lying on their stomachs on the seat of a chair. The chair supports the body so the arms and legs can pretend to swim. Challenge the learners to make a variety of strokes and speeds.

STRETCH B: NOODLE KNOCKOUT

Materials Needed: Two or more pool noodles

Play with the pool noodles and pretend to duel. Allow learners to take turns in pairs or play in a large group. Establish good boundaries before beginning the activity. Explain that the noodles are to hit only noodles—not people. Caution the children to keep the noodles away from faces. Make sure an adult is close by during this activity to monitor and enforce safety.

STRETCH C: RAIN GUTTER RACES

Materials: Two new gutters with waterproof coverings on ends, water, balloons, straws (optional)

Fill each gutter with water. Blow up and tie off balloons (small enough to fit inside the gutter). Set the gutters on a low table or on a hard floor.

Two learners at a time will race to see who can send their balloon "boats" to the end of the gutter first. Each child places a balloon at the starting end of the gutter. Say, **On your mark! Get ready! Get set! Go!** Both children blow their balloon boats (with or without a straw) until reaching the end of the gutter. The first child to finish wins that round.

Station 1: Games (Choose One)

A. DRIP, DRIP, DROP

Prep: You will need a plastic pitcher and a garden hose (or a trash can filled with water). This is best played as an outdoor game, with the children in swimsuits.

THE GROUND WILL BECOME WET AND SLIPPERY. REMIND CHILDREN TO BE CAREFUL—YOU MAY CHOOSE TO WALK INSTEAD OF RUN.

Steps: This game is played similar to Duck, Duck, Goose. Children sit in a circle and one child is chosen to be "It." This child gets a pitcher full of water and walks behind the circle with the pitcher. As "It" passes each person seated in the circle, he or she drips a tiny amount of water on each head and says, "Drip!" When "It" wants to initiate a chase, he or she pours the contents of the pitcher on another child's head and shouts, "Drop!" The wet child chases "It" around the circle. "It" must sit down in the vacated seat before being tagged. If "It" makes it around the circle and sits down, the wet child becomes the new "It." If "It" is tagged, he or she remains "It" and tries again.

Variation: If children do not have swimsuits on today, play a modified game by using a squirt bottle that sprays a mist. Then as the child goes around, she or he can give pretend squirts to one or two persons and then actually "mist" the one who will give chase.

Spiritual Application: Ask the children what they think this game teaches them about God and endurance. Accept any answer as positive! Then say, **Sometimes we don't have a lot of things dumped on us—maybe little drips of hard times or little drips like bad days. But sometimes we have stuff dropped on us that is very hard—someone is sick or our dog dies. In all situations we still need to press on toward the goal and strain toward what is ahead.**

B. WATER BALLOON TOSS

Prep: Fill up water balloons with water before the session begins and put them in a big tub or the swimming pool used in the Bible lesson.

Steps: Learners will choose partners. One partner will be "A" and the other "B." All the A partners should stand in one line and their B partners stand across from them in another line. Give all the A partners a water balloon. Say, **On your mark! Get Ready! Get Set! Go!** All throw the balloons to their partners at the same time. Any pair who drops a balloon is out of the game. Any pair whose balloon does not break stays in the game. Line B takes a step backward, and the process is repeated until only one pair remains.

Variation: Play hot potato with a water balloon. When the music stops, whoever is holding the water balloon gets to break it on his or her head (or in a bucket).

Spiritual Application: Allow the learners to share how they think this game teaches them about God and endurance. **You still played the game even though you knew at some point you could get wet! Playing the game was worth the risk of getting wet. Think about this: Following Jesus is worth the risk of having a bad day or going through hard times.** Allow the children to elaborate.

C. BEACH OBSTACLE COURSE

Prep: Provide beach balls, hula hoops, kiddie pools, pool noodles, and life jackets. Set up an obstacle course in any order you choose. A part of the obstacle course may include passing the beach ball down the line of your entire team; two people might hula-hoop ten times each; someone might run around the kiddie pool five times; someone might jump over five pool noodles in a row; everyone might swim still in chairs (see Warm-Ups) for twenty-five strokes; someone might put a life jacket on all the way and quote the unit memory verses before taking the jacket off.

Steps: Regardless of how you set up the course, include a "turnaround" in the path where the learners will come back toward where they started. Explain the rules, divide into teams, and begin. If the group is small, they might go one at a time through the course.

Spiritual Application: Reinforce the part of Philippians 3:13 that says "forgetting what is behind." Explain that turnarounds are important in life—and that the children will be talking more about this toward the end of the session.

Station 2: Crafts (Choose One)

A. Life Jackets

Supplies: Brown paper grocery sacks (one for each child), orange paint and paintbrushes or markers, scissors, white ribbon (one to two inches wide), prepared mailing labels with session verses printed on them

Steps: To save time, you may want to cut each bag into "vests" prior to the session. Cut as follows: (1) Cut a straight line up the center of the front of the sack (from the open end to the folded end). (2) From the cut straight line, cut a circle in the bottom of the sack. (3) Cut armholes in the two narrow sides of the sack.

Give each child a precut paper sack or help the learners cut the holes in the sacks themselves. The older children can help the younger ones with this task. Paint the sacks orange or color with markers. (Variation: Glue orange pieces of paper on the bag instead of painting or coloring.) Attach the mailing labels. Attach white ribbon ties with staples. The students might also write the other key words from *God's Olympics* on different areas of their jackets. Once the paint is dry, learners can wear the life jackets.

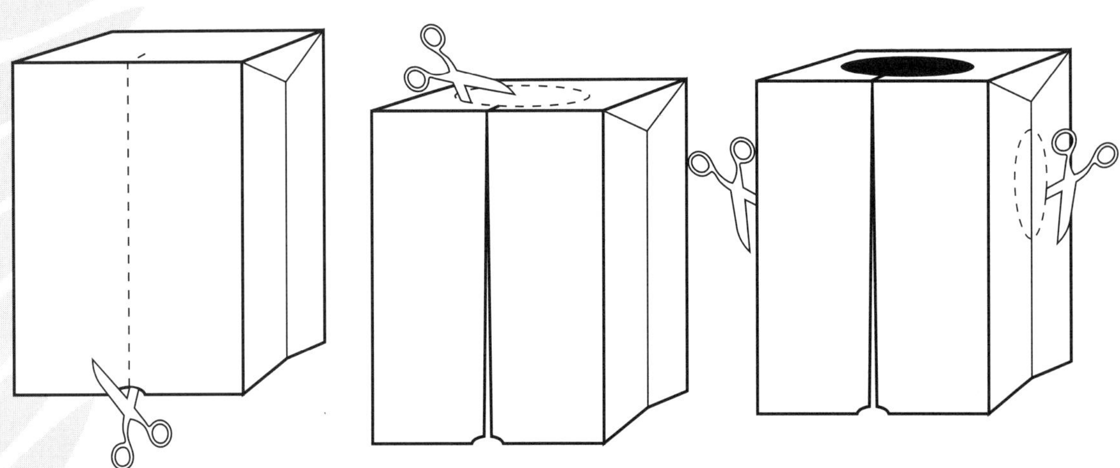

ANY COLOR CRAYON WILL WORK, BUT WHITE STANDS OUT BEST IN A RESIST PAINTING.

B. Underwater Words

Supplies: White crayons, white card stock or paper, blue watercolor paint, paintbrushes

Steps: Write the session verses on the board or a poster. Instruct the students to copy the verses on paper with a white crayon. Paint over the words with blue watercolor paint. Anything written in crayon will resist the paint. If there is time, encourage the students to color with a white crayon a picture of their favorite activity during all of *God's Olympics* and then paint it with blue watercolor. Take turns sharing what the students have learned about God through their favorite activities.

Station 3: Snacks (Choose One)

A. Make: Beach Towel Crackers

Ingredients: Graham crackers, icing in a variety of colors, plastic knives

Steps: Put two or three plastic knives in each color of icing. Give all learners a plate and a graham cracker. Decorate the graham crackers like beach towels and enjoy!

B. Serve (Make Ahead): Fishbowl

Several hours before the session, make blue Jell-O and pour into small, clear cups. Add gummy fish to the blue Jell-O and then chill thoroughly. Make one cup per child.

C. Serve: Goldfish and Lifesavers

Offer the children fish-shaped crackers and ocean water (any juice or ice water). Also give a LifeSaver candy to each child.